PHONICS

Grade 3

Printed in the U.S.A.

ISBN 978-0-544-26776-3

5 6 7 8 9 10   0982   22 21 20 19 18 17 16 15

4500571485   A B C D E F G

Core Skills Phonics

Grade 3

Unit 1: Consonants

Unit 2: Short and Long Vowels

Unit 3: Consonant Blends and Digraphs, Syllables, Silent Consonants

Unit 4: *r*-Controlled Vowels, *y* as a Vowel, Schwa, Vowel and Digraphs, Diphthongs

Table of Contents
Core Skills Phonics, Grade 3

Features

The *Core Skills Phonics* series provides skill-specific pages that link phonics with spelling and reading, allowing students to build language skills through integrated activities.

In *Core Skills Phonics*, you will find two-page lessons that provide ample opportunity to practice one specific phonics skill.

The **skill box** explains the rule and cites examples.

Exercises allow students to use visual and auditory modalities to explore the skill.

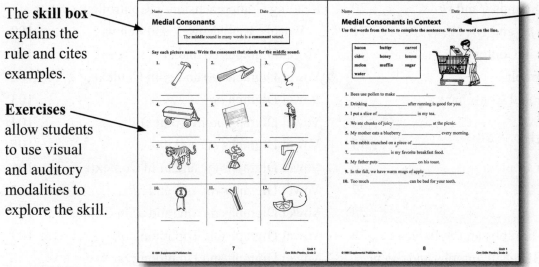

A **context** activity gives students additional practice in reading words with the phonics skill.

Other features include the following:

- periodic **reviews** in each unit to ensure that students have mastered the skill.

- a **passage** at the end of each unit, which contains phonics-based words, to develop reading comprehension.

- **Quiz Yourself!**, an informal test of students' knowledge of the unit skills.

- a **unit assessment** to determine if students have mastered the phonics skills.

- a **general assessment**, found on pages 1 and 2, which can be used as a diagnostic tool to gauge students' phonics knowledge before instruction or as a final test.

General Assessment

Circle the missing letter. Write the letter to complete the word.

1.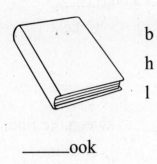

b

h

l

_____ook

2.

r

x

t

si_____

3.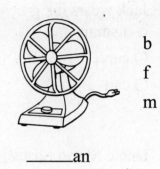

b

f

m

_____an

Circle the word that names each picture.

4.

mom

man

mop

5.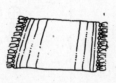

run

rude

rug

6.

sun

soap

sum

7.

tree

creep

try

8.

blink

glove

drove

9.

laugh

fluff

log

10.

course

coins

cruise

11.

clown

clock

down

12.

dear

tear

deer

General Assessment, p. 2

Fill in the circle next to the word that completes each sentence.

1. Jack wears his green _____ when it is sunny.
   ○ car   ○ lap
   ○ cap

2. Uncle Mario raises _____ on his ranch.
   ○ goats   ○ gates
   ○ gems

3. I like a sliced _____ with my cereal.
   ○ bakery   ○ banana
   ○ binder

4. Take your _____ and ball home.
   ○ bit   ○ bat
   ○ best

5. We will swim in the _____.
   ○ like   ○ lack
   ○ lake

6. Did you plant a _____ tree?
   ○ pin   ○ pine
   ○ pane

7. I am sick with a bad _____.
   ○ rough   ○ cost
   ○ cough

8. Here's a _____ to sweep the floor.
   ○ stool   ○ drum
   ○ broom

9. Please _____ your hair.
   ○ comb   ○ thumb
   ○ climb

10. You _____ just like your mother.
    ○ look   ○ loud
    ○ lawn

11. Dad dried the cups and _____ with a dish towel.
    ○ saucers   ○ seesaw
    ○ sausage

12. Mr. Goldman has a bushy _____.
    ○ barn   ○ book
    ○ beard

2

Initial Consonants

The **first** sound in many words is a **consonant** sound.

Say each picture name. Write the consonant that stands for the first sound.

1.
_____

2.
_____

3.
_____

4.
_____

5.
_____

6.
_____

7.
_____

8.
_____

9.
_____

10.
_____

11.
_____

12.
_____

Initial Consonants in Context

Circle the word that completes each sentence. Write the word on the line.

1. I like to visit the _____.   park   lark   bark

2. I went there last _____ with my friend.   peak   seek   week

3. The park ranger rode in a _____.   jeep   leap   weep

4. I saw a _____ on the side of a hill.   door   deer   dare

5. Jane fed _____ to a squirrel.   cuts   quits   nuts

6. The _____ would not come out of its shell.   rattle   turtle   bottle

7. I saw a _____ with blue feathers.   best   bell   bird

8. Jane saw a _____ with a yellow stripe.   fish   fur   fry

9. A _____ robin hopped close to me.   hung   young   gong

10. We were very _____ as we watched it.   quiet   kite   diet

Final Consonants

> The **last** sound in many words is a **consonant** sound.

Say each picture name. Write the consonant that stands for the <u>last</u> sound to complete each word.

1. 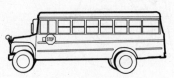 bu_____	2. finge_____	3.  stam_____
4. 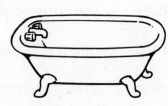 tu_____	5.  be_____	6. 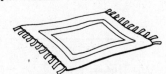 ru_____
7.  swi_____	8. 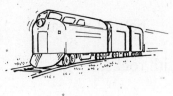 trai_____	9.  do_____
10.  roo_____	11.  goa_____	12. 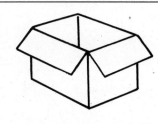 bo_____

Final Consonants in Context

Circle the word that completes each sentence. Write the word on the line.

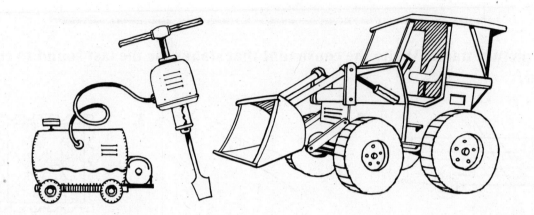

1. I like to visit my dad at _____.   work   wood   worm

2. We drive the _____ to get there.   can   cat   car

3. The _____ is bumpy.   road   roam   roar

4. We listen to _____ on the radio.   moon   must   music

5. The workers _____ a big hole.   did   dim   dig

6. Dad wears a hard _____ on his head.   hat   has   ham

7. He keeps a _____ behind his ear.   pedal   pencil   pepper

8. I fill a _____ with rocks.   box   bog   boy

9. We sit on the _____ and eat our lunch.   grass   grab   grill

10. We watch the workers build a _____.   dam   dab   dad

Medial Consonants

The **middle** sound in many words is a **consonant** sound.

Say each picture name. Write the consonant that stands for the middle sound.

1.
_____

2.
_____

3.
_____

4.
_____

5.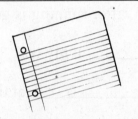
_____

6.
_____

7.
_____

8.
_____

9.
_____

10.
_____

11.
_____

12.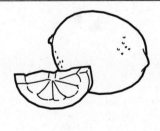
_____

Medial Consonants in Context

Use the words from the box to complete the sentences. Write the word on the line.

bacon	butter	carrot
cider	honey	lemon
melon	muffin	sugar
water		

1. Bees use pollen to make _____.

2. Drinking _____ after running is good for you.

3. I put a slice of _____ in my tea.

4. We ate chunks of juicy _____ at the picnic.

5. My mother eats a blueberry _____ every morning.

6. The rabbit crunched on a piece of _____.

7. _____ is my favorite breakfast food.

8. My father puts _____ on his toast.

9. In the fall, we have warm mugs of apple _____.

10. Too much _____ can be bad for your teeth.

Name _____ Date _____

Review Initial, Final, and Medial Consonants

Say each picture name. Write the missing consonant or consonants to complete each word.

1.  _____un	2.  _____ite	3.  ba_____
4.  _____an	5.  pa_____ot	6.  di_____
7.  ca_____el	8. 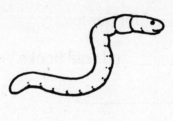 _____orm	9.  _____ell
10.  _____at	11.  bea_____	12. 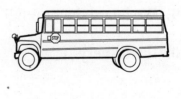 bu_____

Review Initial, Final, and Medial Consonants in Context

Complete each sentence with a word from the box.

cabin	deer
fish	lemon
mug	quiet
roof	sofa
tulip	water

1. Last week, we went to a _____ by the lake.

2. The _____ in the lake was cold.

3. Mom put a pink _____ on the table.

4. She sliced a _____ for our tea.

5. We sat on the _____ and read books.

6. I ate my soup from a _____.

7. We saw many _____ in the woods.

8. Dad caught _____ for dinner.

9. We heard the rain fall on the _____.

10. It was very _____ away from the city.

Hard and Soft *c*

The letter **c** can stand for more than one sound. It can stand for the **hard c** sound you hear in **cat**. **Hard c** sounds like **k**. When **e**, **i**, or **y** comes after **c**, the **c** usually stands for the **soft c** sound you hear in **city**.

cat

city

Read each sentence. Circle the words that contain the letter c. Then write the words with the soft c sound under the city. Write the words with the hard c sound under the cat.

1. I like the city more than the country.

2. It is fun to live in the center of things.

3. It is nice to skate on ice in the park.

4. I can get a taxicab on a corner.

5. I like to see actors in a play.

6. I love living in a big place.

_____   _____

_____   _____

_____   _____

_____   _____

11

Hard and Soft *c* in Context

Use the words from the box to complete each sentence.

call	cat
cob	cub
cent	cider
coat	fence
pencil	voice

1. If you have a penny, you have one _____.

2. The mother bear held her _____.

3. I wear a _____ when it is cold.

4. My _____ likes to sit in the sun.

5. Use a _____ on your test.

6. Speak in a soft _____ in the library.

7. I like warm apple _____ in the fall.

8. _____ your friend on the phone.

9. Corn on the _____ is a healthful food.

10. I will paint the _____ this week.

Hard and Soft *g*

The letter **g** can stand for more than one sound. It can stand for the **hard g** sound you hear in **gate**. When **e**, **i**, or **y** comes after **g**, the **g** stands for the **soft g** sound you hear in **giraffe**. **Soft g** sounds like **j**.

gas

giraffe

Say each picture name. Write the correct word from the box on the line.

dog	flag	gem	gerbil	guitar	igloo	mug	pigeon	tiger

1. _____

2. _____

3. _____

4. _____

5. _____

6. _____

7. _____

8. _____

9. _____

13

Hard and Soft *g* in Context

Complete each sentence with a word from the box. Write the word on the line.

cage	game
gentle	giant
giraffe	gold
gym	huge
pigeon	sugar

1. I love to play in the _____ on rainy days.

2. All morning, we wait to play a _____.

3. I pretend I am a tall _____ at the zoo.

4. I am the _____ of the zoo.

5. I am slow and _____ when I walk.

6. My feet are _____!

7. I pretend my hair is _____ with brown spots.

8. I like to eat _____ from the zookeeper's hand.

9. Sometimes, a _____ will land on my head.

10. I am too big to live in a _____.

Name _____ Date _____

Variant *s*

The letter **s** can stand for more than one sound. It can stand for the **s** sound you hear in **sock** and the **z** sound you hear in **rose**. The letter **s** and the letters **ss** can also stand for the **sh** sound you hear in **sugar** and **tissue**.

sock   rose   sugar   tissue

Say each picture name. Write the sound the s̱ stands for—s̱, ẕ, or s̱ẖ—on the line. Then circle the word or words that have s̱ in each sentence.

 _____

1. Keep a tissue in your pocket.

 _____

2. Make sure you come home on time.

3. Mom will serve me soup and salad.

4. Sandy is too sick to go outside.

 _____

5. Use your nose to find the rose.

6. He likes peas and beans and french fries.

**Find the word in the box that completes each sentence.
Write the word on the line.**

7. Sam knows how to make his favorite _____.

8. He puts _____ on some bread.

9. His mom grills the food and serves it for _____.

10. Sam is _____ that his mom is the best cook.

cheese
sandwich
supper
sure

Core Skills Phonics, Grade 3

Variant *s* in Context

Circle the words that have <u>s</u> in each sentence. Then write each word in the correct column.

1. Dan assured me that he has many favorite books.

2. He read one about a space mission.

3. He used a tissue when he read about the sad prince.

4. We both like books about country music.

5. I was sure he would like a book about leaves.

6. I gave it to him as a present.

<u>s</u> sound of <u>s</u>	<u>z</u> sound of <u>s</u>	<u>sh</u> sound of <u>s</u>
_____	_____	_____
_____	_____	_____
_____	_____	_____
	_____	
	_____	
	_____	

Review Variant *c*, *g*, and *s*

Say each picture name. Write the missing consonant or consonants on the line.

1.  _____andle	2.  _____old	3. chee_____e
4. _____em	5.  _____ent	6. _____ugar
7.  pre_____ent	8.  ho_____e	9.  ti_____ue

Use a word from the box to answer each riddle.

10. Which word means "an animal with a hump on its back"?

_____

11. Which word equals 3 + 4? _____

12. What is another word for "automobile"? _____

13. What falls off a tree in autumn? _____

14. Which word means "a house made of ice"? _____

camel

car

leaves

seven

igloo

Unit 1
Core Skills Phonics, Grade 3

Review Variant *c, g,* and *s*: Hidden Words

Each word in the box is in the puzzle. Find and circle each word. Then color words with hard or soft c red, words with hard or soft g blue, and words with s green. Words go across, down, at a slant, and backwards.

gorilla	center	color	dance	sink
baseball	rose	giraffe	goat	museum
ice	sure	solve	gem	dinosaur

```
s   a   u   l   o   e   c   r   g   e   t   g

e   s   m   a   s   r   i   e   c   g   r   i

k   o   i   o   t   i   o   n   a   o   j   r

l   l   r   n   e   i   a   p   g   r   d   a

y   v   e   s   k   d   i   c   e   i   i   f

r   e   m   u   s   e   u   m   m   l   n   f

c   b   b   a   g   o   t   t   u   l   o   e

e   s   o   m   c   o   l   o   r   a   s   s

n   g   l   l   a   b   e   s   a   b   a   r

t   v   o   q   c   i   e   d   e   z   u   e

e   w   t   a   r   s   u   r   e   x   r   m

r   b   o   s   t   o   a   w   m   b   p   e
```

18

Review Variant *c*, *g*, and *s* in Context

Circle the words that have c or g in each sentence. Then write each word in the correct column.

1. I like to curl up with my favorite books.

2. One is about a big cat that skates on ice.

3. Another one is about a gentle giant who plays golf.

4. I am certain that I will always love to read.

hard c	soft c	hard g	soft g
_____	_____	_____	_____
_____	_____	_____	_____

Find the word in the box that completes each sentence. Write the word on the line.

5. I like to ride the _____ to the zoo.

6. I learn many _____ about nature.

7. The striped _____ is from Africa.

8. The _____ lives in the ocean and has big tusks.

9. There is a picnic area with a _____.

10. Dad cooks hot dogs, but I like my _____ dog better.

| bus |
| grill |
| lessons |
| corn |
| walrus |
| tiger |

Core Skills Phonics, Grade 3

Reading Comprehension: Variant *c*, *g*, and *s*

Read the story. Then read the sentences below it. Write the word that completes each sentence on the line.

Mice or Gerbils?

Carrie went to the pet shop. She could not decide whether to buy gerbils or mice. Carrie got books on mice and books on gerbils. This is what she learned about them.

Mice and gerbils are both rodents. They are born blind and without fur. Their eyes open soon after they are born. They grow a coat of soft fur, too. Gerbils are fully grown when they are about twelve weeks old. Mice are grown at about six weeks.

A mouse's tail is longer than the rest of its body. Most of the tail is bare. A long, bare tail can help keep the animal cool. A gerbil's furry tail is as long as its body. It uses its tail for balance when it jumps.

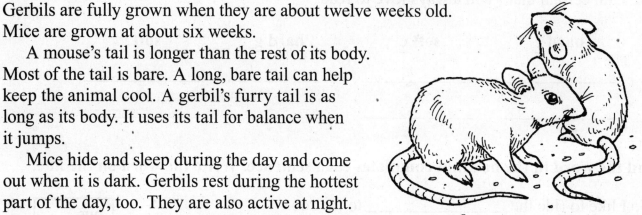

Mice hide and sleep during the day and come out when it is dark. Gerbils rest during the hottest part of the day, too. They are also active at night.

1. Gerbils and mice are both _____.

2. A _____ uses its tail when it jumps.

3. Mice _____ during the day.

4. Both gerbils and mice are _____ at night.

5. A long, bare tail helps keep a mouse _____.

Unit 1
Core Skills Phonics, Grade 3

Quiz Yourself!

Circle the missing letter. Write the letter to complete the word.

1.

f

x

r

bo_____er

2.

t

m

p

ha_____

3.
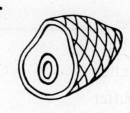

g

d

m

ha_____

4.

t

f

g

wa_____er

5.

h

g

p

_____em

6.

m

k

v

le_____on

7.

t

k

c

mi_____e

8.

r

b

g

ca_____in

9.
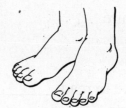

f

r

b

_____eet

10.

g

d

m

mu_____

11.

t

r

s

ho_____e

12.

b

c

h

_____at

Quiz Yourself!, p. 2

Fill in the circle next to the word that completes each sentence. Write the word on the line.

1. I like _____ on a hot muffin.
   ○ butter ○ bumper
   ○ buffer

2. Susan wears _____ ribbons in her hair.
   ○ gold ○ cold
   ○ sold

3. I am _____ that soccer is my favorite sport.
   ○ cure ○ lure
   ○ sure

4. I like to read _____ about sports.
   ○ nooks ○ hooks
   ○ books

5. My mom likes a _____ of hot tea on a cold morning.
   ○ mug ○ mutt
   ○ mud

6. My dad likes to get up early to watch the sun _____.
   ○ rice ○ ripe
   ○ rise

7. Tom likes to read the front _____ of the newspaper.
   ○ pale ○ page
   ○ pace

8. We like to spend the night in a _____ in the woods.
   ○ camel ○ cabin
   ○ candle

9. I often drink _____ after playing outside.
   ○ water ○ wager
   ○ wader

10. One _____ does not buy much.
    ○ rent ○ bent
    ○ cent

Name _____   Date _____

Unit 1 Assessment

Circle the missing letter. Write the letter to complete the word.

1.

    f
    m
    s

_____ilk

2.

    c
    d
    r

_____ity

3.

    r
    f
    l

_____ake

4.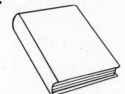

    b
    h
    l

_____ook

5.

    g
    m
    t

hu_____

6.

    s
    r
    l

finge_____

7.

    c
    b
    t

_____ent

8.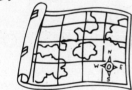

    r
    x
    t

si_____

9.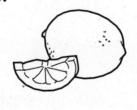

    p
    n
    d

ma_____

10.

    r
    g
    m

le_____on

11.

    b
    f
    m

_____an

12.

    d
    f
    b

_____ad

23

Name _____   Date _____

Unit 1 Assessment, p. 2

Fill in the circle next to the word that completes each sentence.

1. I used a _____ to wipe my face.
   - ○ issue   ○ tissue
   - ○ sugar

2. I can read my sister's favorite _____.
   - ○ book   ○ belt
   - ○ took

3. There is a _____ tree in our backyard.
   - ○ germ   ○ gem
   - ○ giant

4. Jack wears his green _____ when it is sunny.
   - ○ car   ○ lap
   - ○ cap

5. We always watch the _____ at the zoo.
   - ○ meals   ○ seals
   - ○ deals

6. I like to _____ the ducks at the pond.
   - ○ weep   ○ feed
   - ○ need

7. Our family stays in a _____ every summer.
   - ○ carpet   ○ carton
   - ○ cabin

8. My aunt wants to grow _____ in her garden.
   - ○ socks   ○ hoses
   - ○ roses

9. Uncle Mario raises _____ on his ranch.
   - ○ goats   ○ gates
   - ○ gems

10. We saw three clowns at the _____.
    - ○ circus   ○ cabin
    - ○ city

11. Dad cooks soup in a _____.
    - ○ pig   ○ pat
    - ○ pot

12. I like a sliced _____ with my cereal.
    - ○ bakery   ○ banana
    - ○ binder

24

Short Vowel *a*

If a word has only one vowel, the vowel sound is usually short.
Short a is the vowel sound you hear in **map**.

Say each picture name. If the word has the <u>short a</u> sound, write <u>a</u> to complete the word.

1.

b____g

2.

d____d

3.

p____n

4.

c____t

5.

v____t

6.

p____n

7.

d____m

8.

f____n

9.

g____s

10.

c____n

11.

m____p

12.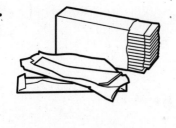

g____m

Short Vowel *a* in Context

Circle the word that completes each sentence. Write the word on the line.

1. Jan and her dad will _____ in the winter.   camp   cone

2. They _____ warm blankets.   pad   pack

3. Dad puts food in a big _____.   bag   bug

4. Then they load the _____.   van   vat

5. Dad stops to get some _____.   gag   gas

6. He looks at his _____, too.   mop   map

7. Dad drives _____ drives all day.   end   and

8. They _____ by towns and farms.   pass   pat

9. Finally, Jan and her dad are _____ the cabin.   it   at

10. Winter _____ come to the woods.   has   his

Short Vowel *o*

If a word has only one vowel, the vowel sound is usually short.
Short o is the vowel sound you hear in **fox**.

fox

Circle the word that names each picture. Write the word on the line.

1. 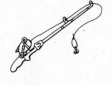 rod rid red _____	**2.**  jig jog jug _____	**3.**  cat cut cot _____
4. log lost lock _____	**5.** pit pot pat _____	**6.** dog dot doll _____
7. 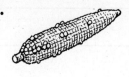 cot cob cod _____	**8.** top tip tap _____	**9.** sick sock sack _____
10. click cluck clock _____	**11.** map mom mop _____	**12.**  hog hug hag _____

Short Vowel *o* in Context

People have often made up stories to explain why things happen. Read each story title. Underline the word that has the <u>short o</u> sound. Write the word on the line.

1. Why the Rabbit Likes to Hop   _____

2. Why Dogs and Cats Fight   _____

3. Why the Sun Is So Hot   _____

4. Why Peas Have Pods   _____

5. Why the Leopard Has Spots   _____

6. Why Ants Crawl on Logs   _____

7. Why the Fox Has a Bushy Tail   _____

8. Why Fish Live in Ponds   _____

9. Why Hogs Like Mud   _____

10. Why Clocks Have Hands   _____

Name _____   Date _____

Short Vowel *i*

If a word has only one vowel, the vowel sound is usually short.
Short i is the vowel sound you hear in **fish**.

fish

Say each picture name. Write the word on the line.

1.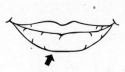
   _____

2.
   _____

3.
   _____

4.
   _____

5.
   _____

6.
   _____

7.
   _____

8.
   _____

9.
   _____

10.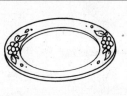
    _____

11.
    _____

12.
    _____

Short Vowel *i* in Context

Read the poem. Underline the words that have the <u>short i</u> sound. Write the words on the lines below.

Have You Ever Wondered . . .

What it's like to be a fish
And give your tail a little swish?
To swim with your fins and dive and dip
And through the water quickly zip?

Do you ever wish…
You could roll and flip?
Or zoom and chase a ship?
To eat from the sea and not a dish?
Oh, how I'd love to be a fish!

1. _____ 2. _____ 3. _____ 4. _____

5. _____ 6. _____ 7. _____ 8. _____

9. _____ 10. _____ 11. _____ 12. _____

13. _____ 14. _____ 15. _____ 16. _____

Short Vowel *u*

If a word has only one vowel, the vowel sound is usually short.
Short u is the vowel sound you hear in **cup**.

cup

Say each picture name. If the word has the <u>short u</u> sound, write <u>u</u> to complete the word.

1.	2.	3.
b_____d	c_____b	f_____n

4.	5.	6.
p_____g	r_____n	j_____g

7.	8.	9.
h_____g	l_____g	p_____p

 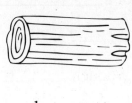

Read each sentence. Find the word in dark print. Replace the vowel to make a <u>short u</u> sound. Write the new word on the line.

10. I wonder how **big** a _____ can get.

11. I wonder how to make _____ out of **rags**.

12. We will need _____ to get this **lock** open.

Short Vowel *u* in Context

Complete each sentence with a word from the box. Write the word on the line.

brush	bug
bus	buzz
cub	duck
run	sun
trunk	tub

Would it be funny if . . .

1. we rode in a balloon instead of a _____?

2. a _____ said "oink" instead of "quack"?

3. the _____ was blue and the sky was yellow?

4. your mother brought home a little bear _____?

5. you had to use a comb to _____ your teeth?

6. an elephant had a nose instead of a _____?

7. all the bees refused to _____?

8. you had to take a bath in a big, wooden _____?

9. every _____ was as big as a car?

10. a snail could _____ as fast as a horse?

Short Vowel e

> If a word has only one vowel, the vowel sound is usually short.
> **Short e** is the vowel sound you hear in **bed**.

bed

Circle the word that names each picture. Write the word on the line.

1.	vast vest vote	2.	net not nut	3. 	tin tan ten
_____		_____		_____	
4.	pit pot peg	5.	bill bell bull	6. 	pen pan pin
_____		_____		_____	

Say each picture name. If the word has the _short e_ sound, write the word on the line.

7.	8. 	9. 
_____	_____	_____
10. 	11.	12. 
_____	_____	_____

Short Vowel *e* in Context

**Read each group of sentences. Complete each sentence with a word at the right.
Write the word on the line.**

1. Do you know how to care for a _____?   went

   Pretend a puppy _____ home with you.   pet

   Here is a _____ of puppy tips.   set

2. First, _____ some puppy food at the store.   fed

   A good brand might have meat and _____ in it.   get

   A puppy can be _____ three small meals a day.   eggs

3. Teach your puppy to behave _____.   well

   Say "No!" _____ your puppy makes a mistake.   when

   Never _____ at your puppy.   yell

4. You can _____ your puppy learn tricks.   end

   Take one _____ at a time.   help

   Say "Good dog!" at the _____ of the day.   step

Review Short Vowels

Say each picture name. Write the word on the line.

1.

_____

2.

_____

3.

_____

4.

_____

5.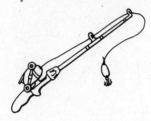

_____

6.

_____

7.

_____

8.

_____

9.

_____

10.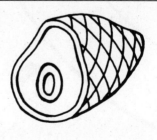

_____

11.

_____

12.

_____

Review Short Vowels: Word Wheel

Start with cat. Change one letter to make a new word that names a picture on the page. Write it in the space next to cat. Repeat these steps to fill the circle. Use each picture name only once.

Review Short Vowels in Context

Complete each sentence with a word from the box.

camp	cot	fan	fun
ham	hit	hop	net
sack	step	sun	swim

1. It's time to go to summer _____.

2. Do you wonder why I have _____ there?

3. It's because the _____ shines every day.

4. My cabin has a _____ to cool us off.

5. We often have a _____ race in the morning.

6. We each _____ into a big bag.

7. Then we see who can _____ the farthest.

8. Later, we go to the court to _____ some tennis balls.

9. We try to get the balls to go over the _____.

10. At lunch, we have _____ and cheese sandwiches.

11. We rest for an hour before we _____ in the lake.

12. Every night, I go to sleep on my _____.

Reading Comprehension: Short Vowels

Read the passage. Then read the sentences below it. Write the word that completes each sentence on the line.

Fizz! Pop! Yum!

Did you ever wonder how soda pop was first made? Long ago, people drank spring water. They thought it kept them from getting sick. Some spring water has carbon dioxide in it. This is a harmless gas that makes water fizz. People liked the fizzy spring water, so scientists tried to make it in labs.

In 1767, Dr. Joseph Priestley added baking soda to plain water. The drink was just like fizzy spring water, so it was called carbonated water.

Soon, drugstores sold carbonated water as a health drink. A cork in the top of each bottle kept the fizz in the water. The cork made a popping sound when it was pulled out. People began to call the drink "pop." Soon people could buy pop in flavors such as lemon, lime, grape, and cherry.

1. Some people thought spring water _____ them healthy.

2. Carbon dioxide is a _____.

3. Dr. Joseph Priestley _____ baking soda to water to make it fizz.

4. Carbonated water was first sold in _____.

5. A cork was put in the _____ of each bottle.

Long Vowel *a*

A vowel usually has the long sound when a consonant and **e** come after it. The **e** is silent.

When two vowels are together, the first vowel usually has the long sound. The second vowel is silent.

You can hear the **long a** sound in **rake**, **nail**, and **hay**.

    rake   nail   hay

Say each picture name. Complete the word if it has the <u>long a sound</u>.

1. 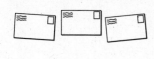	2. 	3. 	4. 
m_____l	c_____n_____	p_____ _____	c_____p
5. 	6.	7. 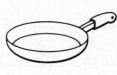	8. 
l_____k_____	p_____ _____l	p_____n	r_____ _____n
9. 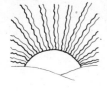	10. 	11. 	12. 
r_____ _____	c_____t	b_____ _____t	s_____ _____l

Long Vowel *a* in Context

Find the word in the box that completes each question. Write the word on the line.

cake	cane
clay	hay
jay	lake
mane	paint
rays	snails

1. How much _____ does an elephant eat in a day?

2. Why is a blue _____ a bossy bird?

3. How much rain does it take to fill a _____?

4. Why does a _____ rise as it bakes?

5. How long does it take to _____ the White House?

6. Are some _____ slower than others?

7. Who made the first candy _____?

8. Why does a lion have a _____?

9. What makes pieces of _____ stick together?

10. How far do the sun's _____ travel into space?

Long Vowel *o*

> A vowel usually has the long sound when a consonant and **e** come after it. The **e** is silent.
>
> When two vowels are together, the first vowel usually has the long sound. The second vowel is silent.
>
> You can hear the **long o** sound in **bone**, **coat**, and **bowl**.

bone   **coat**   **bowl**

Circle each <u>long o</u> word in the box. Write the word that names each picture.

boat	box	cot	crow	dome	goal	got	hot	mop	mow
nose	pot	rod	rope	row	soap	toast	toad	toe	top

1.
_____

2.
_____

3.
_____

4.
_____

5.
_____

6.
_____

7.
_____

8.
_____

9.
_____

10.
_____

11.
_____

12.
_____

Unit 2
Core Skills Phonics, Grade 3

Long Vowel *o* in Context

What did Kate do at school today? Read each sentence to find out. Circle the words with the <u>long o</u> sound. Write the words on the lines.

1. Kate dressed for her show and had some toast.

   _____   _____

2. Her mother loaned her a fancy red bow.

   _____   _____

3. Kate rode the bus from her home to school.

   _____   _____

4. At school, Kate sang a song about a toad and a mole.

   _____   _____

5. She tapped her toes and sang a high note.

   _____   _____

6. She waved a rose and sang a very low note.

   _____   _____   _____

7. Then she made a joke about a frog in her throat.

   _____   _____

8. Everyone clapped so much that Kate's face glowed with pride.

   _____   _____

Long Vowel *i*

A vowel usually has the long sound when a consonant and **e** come after it. The **e** is silent.

When two vowels are together, the first vowel usually has the long sound. The second vowel is silent.

When the vowel **i** is followed by **gh**, the **i** usually has the long sound. The **g** and **h** are silent.

You can hear the **long i** sound in **kite**, **tie**, and **light**.

k**i**te

t**ie**

l**igh**t

Circle the word that names each picture. Write the word on the line.

1.
pipe
pig
pine
_____

2.
pile
pipe
pie
_____

3.
hill
hike
hitch
_____

4.
nail
night
nice
_____

5.
bit
boat
bike
_____

6.
die
did
dice
_____

7.
vet
vine
visit
_____

8.
smell
smile
sun
_____

9.
tie
tip
tide
_____

Long Vowel *i* in Context

Find the word in the box that answers each question. Write the word on the line.

dime	ice
lime	mice
night	pie
prize	right
sigh	tight

1. What coin is worth ten cents? _____

2. What is the opposite of day? _____

3. What is another word for "correct"? _____

4. What is more than one mouse? _____

5. What is the opposite of loose? _____

6. What is a sound you might make when you're sad? _____

7. What kind of dessert has a crust? _____

8. What is something you win? _____

9. What is a name for a kind of green fruit? _____

10. What is frozen water? _____

Long Vowel *u*

A vowel usually has the long sound when a consonant and **e** come after it. The **e** is usually silent.

When two vowels are together, the first vowel usually has the long sound. The second vowel is usually silent.

You can hear the **long u** sound in **cube**, **flute**, and **glue**.

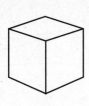

cube

flute

glue

Say each picture name. Complete the word if it has the long u sound.

1.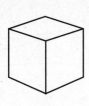

   t____b____

2.

   t____n____

3.

   c____b

4.

   pl____m____

5.

   r____l____r

6.

   b____g

7.

   m____l____

8.

   h____g

9.

   gl____ ____

10.

    fl____t____

11.

    d____ck

12.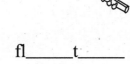

    f____s____

Long Vowel *u* in Context

The underlined word in each sentence does not make sense. Find the word in the box that does make sense. Write the word on the line. <u>Hint:</u> **The correct word begins like the underlined word.**

blue	clue
cube	cute
glue	huge
June	Luke
mule	use

1. Sue and <u>Like</u> want to put on a show.   _____

2. At first, they don't have a <u>clap</u> how to begin.   _____

3. They wonder what to <u>unit</u> for a stage.   _____

4. Then Sue finds a <u>hope</u> box.   _____

5. It is shaped like a <u>cab</u>.   _____

6. Sue covers the box with a <u>blow</u> cloth.   _____

7. Sue and Luke use <u>glow</u> to make masks.   _____

8. Sue is a bear with a <u>cave</u> face.   _____

9. Luke is a funny <u>mail</u>.   _____

10. All the children come to watch them on one <u>Josh</u> day.   _____

Long Vowel e

When two vowels are together, the first vowel usually has the long sound. The second vowel is silent. You can hear the **long e** sound in **leaf** and **bee**.

leaf   bee

Circle the word that names each picture. Write the word on the line.

1.  ten / team / tea	2. send / soap / seed	3.  pest / peas / past
4. knew / kneel / knee	5. peach / peek / pack	6. meet / meal / meat
7. bend / bean / beak	8. weak / went / weed	9. quiet / queen / quit
10. 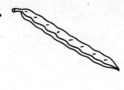 fell / fear / feet	11. seal / seem / sell	12. left / leaf / lean

Unit 2
Core Skills Phonics, Grade 3

Long Vowel e in Context

Read each sentence and the words below it. Write the two words that will complete the sentence.

1. What will _____ _____ at the park?

   Lee   bean   see

2. Whom will he _____ on the _____?

   street   meet   wheat

3. A man drives by in a _____ _____.

   jeep   sweep   neat

4. A _____ buzzes in a _____.

   peace   bee   tree

5. Birds in a nest _____ and _____.

   beet   cheep   peep

6. Two girls _____ a picnic _____.

   meal   eat   beak

7. Lee buys a _____ _____.

   weak   treat   sweet

8. Lee _____ his friend _____.

   sees   Neal   seal

9. They _____ to _____ the ducks.

   need   feed   leap

10. Lee and Neal will _____ at the park next _____.

    week   seem   meet

Core Skills Phonics, Grade 3

Review Long Vowels

Find the word in the box that names each picture. Write the word on the line.

beak	bee	bike	dune	flute	glue
hose	nail	nine	tape	toad	wheel

1.

_____

2.

_____

3.

_____

4.

_____

5.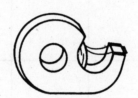

_____

6.

_____

7.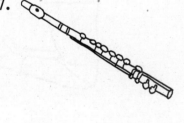

_____

8.

_____

9.

_____

10.

_____

11.

_____

12.

_____

Review Long Vowels: Vowel Tic-Tac-Toe

In each grid, circle the three words in a row that have the same vowel sound. Words may go across, down, or diagonally. Then make your own tic-tac-toe puzzle by filling in the empty grid with words of your own. Have a partner solve the puzzle.

1.

cap	pail	fat
game	nail	name
mail	hand	man

2.

men	pea	let
tree	bean	bee
ten	red	peek

3.

mud	fuse	cube
cut	tune	flute
blue	tug	pup

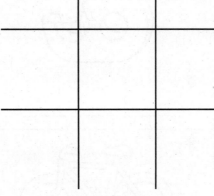

4.

pop	cold	bone
toe	roll	stop
lot	goat	mom

5.

dig	find	pin
hide	light	bite
ripe	kit	rip

6.

hot	rock	cold
bowl	box	dog
post	hold	dome

Review Long Vowels in Context

Read each sentence. Unscramble the words in dark print. Write the correct word on the line. The words in the box may help you.

blue	bone	jay	jeep	kite	lime
midnight	pane	queen	tie	tube	tow

1. I wonder how high I can fly this **tiek**. _____

2. I wonder why a dog likes to chew on a **nebo**. _____

3. I wonder how they get toothpaste into a **bute**. _____

4. I wonder why the sky is **elbu**. _____

5. A **neuqe** sits on a throne and wears a crown. _____

6. Cinderella had to be home by **tignidmh**. _____

7. A **meli** is bright green. _____

8. A **ajy** is a bird with blue feathers. _____

9. Mr. Ono will **wto** our truck to the garage. _____

10. The ball hit the window and broke a **neap**. _____

11. Can you use this ribbon to **ite** a bow? _____

12. The word **epej** rhymes with "sheep". _____

Reading Comprehension: Long Vowels

Brandon wrote a letter to Dr. Helpful. He asked for rules to help him stay healthy. Dr. Helpful answered Brandon's letter. Read Dr. Helpful's letter to Brandon. Then read the sentences below it. Write the word that completes each sentence on the line.

Dear Brandon,

No one feels good all the time. Everyone gets a cold once in a while. Here are some rules to help you. If you follow them, you will feel good most of the time.

First, eat three main meals a day. Choose a wide range of foods. Meat is good for you. You also need to eat lots of leafy green vegetables. It is all right to have fruit for a snack.

Next, you need to keep active. Go outside and play. Skating, riding a bike, and hiking are good kinds of exercise. You can also exercise while you help at home. It takes lots of energy to rake leaves!

Finally, be sure you get a good night's sleep. Rest is important for a growing child.

If you follow these rules, you will have a healthy glow!

Yours in good health,
Dr. I.M. Helpful

1. The doctor gave Brandon a set of _____ to help him stay healthy.

2. Dr. Helpful told Brandon to eat _____ meals a day.

3. A healthful meal has a wide _____ of foods.

4. It is important to eat lots of leafy _____ vegetables.

5. Every _____ needs plenty of rest each night.

Quiz Yourself!

Circle the word that names each picture. Write the word on the line.

1.

can
cane
came

_____

2.

child
chick
chill

_____

3.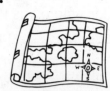

mop
map
man

_____

4.

tape
tap
top

_____

5.

huge
hut
hue

_____

6.

bell
bed
bean

_____

7.

cot
coat
coal

_____

8.

bolt
boat
belt

_____

9.

bit
bake
bike

_____

10.

name
nut
nail

_____

11.

dog
deer
duck

_____

12.

van
vet
vine

_____

Quiz Yourself!, p. 2

Fill in the circle next to the word that completes each sentence. Write the word on the line.

1. I wonder who owns that
   _____ puppy.
   ○ cut   ○ cube
   ○ cute

2. I wonder which _____ is
   best for me.
   ○ pit   ○ pet
   ○ pat

3. Ava's dog always wags his
   _____.
   ○ toad   ○ tag
   ○ tail

4. Would you trade your favorite book
   for a bag of _____?
   ○ cold   ○ most
   ○ gold

5. It's fun to _____ on the
   trail through the woods.
   ○ hike   ○ high
   ○ hit

6. Leave now so that you don't
   _____ the party.
   ○ mitt   ○ miss
   ○ mess

7. Our football _____ won
   the big game.
   ○ team   ○ time
   ○ tent

8. Wear a _____ to keep
   your head warm.
   ○ cup   ○ cat
   ○ cap

9. Be sure to _____ the door
   when you leave.
   ○ luck   ○ lick
   ○ lock

10. I use a _____ to dig in
    the garden.
    ○ hoe   ○ hay
    ○ high

Unit 2 Assessment

Circle the word that names each picture. Write the word on the line.

1.

men
meat
meet

_____

2.

sun
soap
sum

_____

3.

toss
toast
tone

_____

4.

bean
bee
been

_____

5.

vest
vine
vet

_____

6.

fun
fin
fan

_____

7.

nail
nap
nine

_____

8.

mom
man
mop

_____

9.

run
rude
rug

_____

10.

joy
jay
jar

_____

11.

blue
gloom
glue

_____

12.

ten
team
tea

_____

Unit 2 Assessment, p. 2

Fill in the circle next to the word that completes each sentence.

1. Did Dad _____ for the cab ride?
   - ○ pay
   - ○ pan
   - ○ pig

2. I _____ my red cap.
   - ○ load
   - ○ list
   - ○ lost

3. Did you plant a _____ tree?
   - ○ pin
   - ○ pine
   - ○ pane

4. The pond is very _____.
   - ○ duck
   - ○ deep
   - ○ doe

5. He _____ the ball into the seats.
   - ○ hat
   - ○ hut
   - ○ hit

6. I like to help _____ the sheets.
   - ○ feed
   - ○ fun
   - ○ fold

7. Take your _____ and ball home.
   - ○ bit
   - ○ bat
   - ○ best

8. May I _____ your pen?
   - ○ ask
   - ○ use
   - ○ up

9. The _____ feels very hot today.
   - ○ send
   - ○ song
   - ○ sun

10. She went to _____ at nine.
    - ○ bid
    - ○ bed
    - ○ bad

11. We will swim in the _____.
    - ○ like
    - ○ lack
    - ○ lake

12. What should I _____ for the trip?
    - ○ pick
    - ○ pack
    - ○ pace

Initial *s* Blends

A **consonant blend** is two or more consonants that are together. The sounds blend together. Each sound is heard. You can hear an **s** blend at the beginning of **scarf**, **skates**, **smoke**, and **squirrel**.

scarf   **sk**ates   **sm**oke   **squ**irrel

Find the word in the box that names each picture. Write the word on the line. Then circle the <u>s</u> blend in each word.

skunk	smile	snail	snake	spill	smoke
squash	squeeze	star	stove	swim	spot

1.

_____

2.

_____

3.

_____

4.

_____

5.

_____

6.

_____

7.

_____

8.

_____

9.

_____

10.

_____

11.

_____

12.

_____

More Initial *s* Blends

Some **consonant blends** have three consonants. You can hear an **s** blend with three letters at the beginning of **splash** and **string**.

splash

string

Circle the word that names each picture. Write the word on the line.

1. screen scram scream _____	**2.** spray sprout sprite _____	**3.** 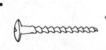 streak straw strange _____
4. screw scrape screech _____	**5.** spring sprain spread _____	**6.** stroll strong string _____

Find the word in the box that completes each sentence. Write the word on the line.

7. I dream about living beside a _____ in the woods.

8. Every afternoon, I would _____ out for a nap.

9. I would find a _____ kitten and take good care of it.

10. I would teach it not to _____ or hiss.

11. We would sit and watch the fish _____.

12. We would see a fish with a black _____ on its side.

scratch
splash
stray
stream
stretch
stripe

Initial *r* Blends

Remember that a **consonant blend** is two or more consonants that are together. You can hear an **r** blend at the beginning of **crab**, **drum**, **frog**, and **grapes**.

crab

drum

frog

grapes

Say each picture name. Write the r blend on the line to complete the word.

1.
____ ____ide

2.
____ ____ow

3.
____ ____ink

4.
____ ____ince

5.
____ ____ave

6.
____ ____ize

7.
____ ____ain

8.
____ ____ill

9.
____ ____idge

10.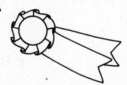
____ ____uit

11.
____ ____ee

12.
____ ____ess

Initial *r* and *s* Blends in Context

Read the story. Find and circle the words that begin with s blends. Next, find and underline the words that begin with r blends. Then, write each word in the correct column.

I dreamed of a special trip with my grandmother. One spring day, we traveled to Spain. People greeted us with smiles. Then, we took a train to a town by a lake. We snacked on grapes. The breeze smelled like flowers! For lunch, we ate spaghetti and meatballs. I wanted to stay, but it was time to go.

s Blends   **r Blends**

_____ _____   _____ _____

_____ _____   _____ _____

_____ _____   _____ _____

_____ _____   _____ _____

Initial *l* and *tw* Blends

Remember that a **consonant blend** is two or more consonants that are together in a word. The sounds blend together, but each sound is heard. You can hear an **l** blend at the beginning of **flag** and a **tw** blend at the beginning of **twelve**.

flag

twelve

The words at the left name the pictures in each row. Write each word under the picture it names. Then circle the l or tw blend in each word.

twins clock glue twenty	1. _____	2. _____	3. _____	4. _____

flower globe plum glass	5. _____	6. _____	7. _____	8. _____

twig cloud plate slide	9. _____	10. _____	11. _____	12. _____

61

Initial *l* and *tw* Blends in Context

Circle the word that completes each sentence. Write the word on the line.

1. I dreamed of soft _____ of snow.   flakes   brakes   cakes

2. Snow fell from gray _____.   loud   blocks   clouds

3. All the children put on their _____.   doves   gloves   globes

4. Each child had a _____ scarf to wear.   blue   glue   clue

5. Everyone had a wooden _____ to ride.   sled   step   led

6. Each child slid down the hill _____.   twig   slice   twice

7. Then, a _____ flew overhead.   plane   plant   pane

8. It dropped _____ lunches for the children.   twist   twelve   train

9. Everyone was _____ to have the wonderful food.   glass   glad   flag

10. They were happy to _____ all day.   play   plate   plum

Final Consonant Blends

A **consonant blend** can also come at the end of a word. You can hear a consonant blend at the end of **lamp** and **list**.

lamp

list

Read each clue and look at the picture. Use a word from the box to complete the answer. Write the word on the line.

| band | cent | lamp | mask | nest | tent | vest | wasp |

1. I make music.

I am a

_____.

2. I am fun to camp in.

I am a

_____.

3. I look good with a shirt.

I am a

_____.

4. I hold a bird's eggs.

I am a

_____.

5. I light up a room.

I am a

_____.

6. I cover a face.

I am a

_____.

7. I am equal to one penny.

I am a

_____.

8. I might sting you.

I am a

_____.

Final Consonant Blends in Context

Circle the word that completes each sentence. Write the word on the line.

1. Trent makes a _____ of jobs he could have when he grows up.

   lisp   list   lies

2. Trent dreams of playing drums in a _____.

   band   bank   back

3. He could wear a _____ if he worked at a lumber mill.

   vent   vet   vest

4. He could also wear a tool _____.

   belt   bell   best

5. When Trent smells the sweet _____ of flowers, he wants to be a florist.

   scent   spent   scene

6. Trent likes to _____, so maybe he'll be a park ranger.

   cast   came   camp

7. Maybe Trent will live in the _____ and ride horses.

   wet   west   went

8. Trent thinks he should _____ his mother for ideas.

   ache   ask   asp

9. His mother holds Trent's _____ in hers.

   had   hand   hang

10. She says, "You have lots of time to find the job that is _____ for you."

    bell   bets   best

Review Initial and Final Consonants

Say each picture name. Write the consonant blend on the line to complete the word.

1.

ce_____

2.

_____ouse

3.

ha_____

4.

____ ____ale

5.

____ ____apes

6.

____ ____ip

7.

____ ____ail

8.

___ ___ ____ing

9.

bi____ ____

10.

____ ____ab

11.

ri____ ____

12.
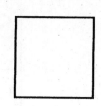
___ ___ ____are

65

Review Initial and Final Consonants:
Don't Spill the Groceries!

Take turns rolling the number cube and moving your marker. Name two words that begin with the blend you land on. If you land on Spill, go back three spaces. If you can't name two words, go back to Start. The first person to reach the Check-Out wins.

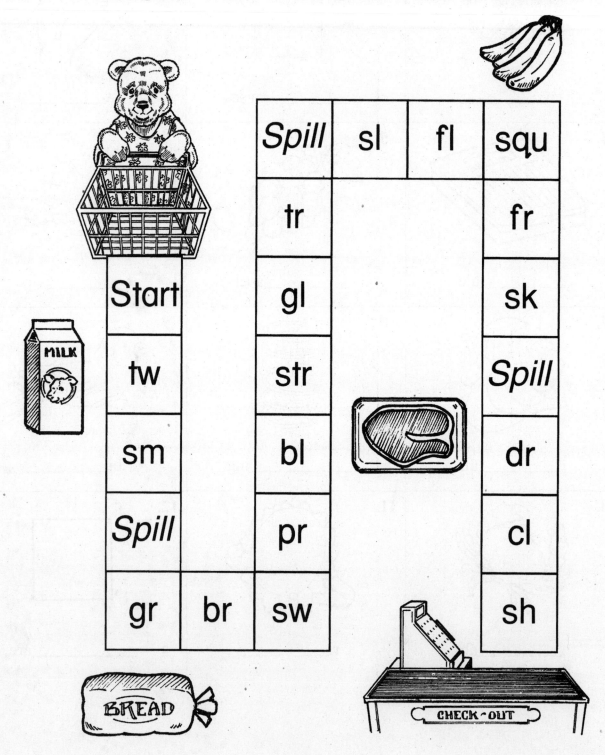

Core Skills Phonics, Grade 3

Review Initial and Final Consonants in Context

**Choose the word that completes each sentence.
Write the word on the line.**

1. The ink made a huge _____ on
   the carpet.

   plain   drain   stain

2. The movie was so sad that I _____ when I saw it.

   tried   cried   pried

3. The moonlight _____ on the water.

   shone   scone   drone

4. Don't _____ others for your mistakes.

   flame   blame   shame

5. Turn on the _____ by the sofa.

   lamp   lamb   laugh

6. It was a _____ to meet the movie star.

   shrill   trill   thrill

7. We saw a _____ of sheep in the meadow.

   flock   clock   crock

8. Please wash your hands in the _____.

   sing   sink   singe

9. There are many large stones and pebbles in that _____.

   stream   scream   dream

10. She wore a blue _____ to the party.

    grass   stress   dress

Reading Comprehension: Initial and Final Consonants

Read the passage. Then read the sentences below it. Write the word that completes each sentence on the line.

Seasons Change

In the winter, the air is cold. We bundle up in our coats and scarves. We sled, skate, and play in the snow. All of the leaves have fallen off the trees, and the tree branches look like twigs.

Then, the air gets warmer. We splash in the rain. Birds start to sing. The ice melts in the streams, and the water flows freely. The plants in Mom's garden begin to grow and blossom. A wren makes her nest in the tree outside my window. Spring has arrived.

In the summer, the weather turns dry and hot. During the day, we swim in the pond and swing on a branch. In the evenings, we sit on the porch and sing while Dad plays the guitar. We water the lawn every five days to keep the grass green.

One day, the wind brings a frost. The trees start to change color, and the plants turn brown. We wear jackets to the football games, and drink hot chocolate in the stands. It is fall.

Soon, snowflakes begin to fall. It is winter again. A change in seasons is great! Don't you agree?

1. In the winter, the tree branches look like _____.

2. Plants grow and birds sing in _____.

3. We water the lawn to keep the _____ green in the summer.

4. The wind brings a _____ at the beginning of fall.

5. A change in seasons is _____!

Consonant Digraphs *ch*, *sh*, *th*, and *wh*

A **consonant digraph** is two or more consonants that are together. They stand for only one sound. You can hear a consonant digraph at the beginning of **chair**, **shoe**, **thumb**, and **whale**.

chair

shoe

thumb

whale

Find the word in the box that names each picture. Write the word on the line. Circle the letters that stand for the <u>first</u> sound in each word.

| thirteen | wheat | sheep | wheel | cheek | ship |

1.

_____

2.

_____

3.

_____

4.

_____

5.

_____

6.

_____

Find the word in the box that completes each sentence. Write the word on the line.

7. I hope I have the _____ to raise horses one day.

8. My horses would have thick, _____ coats.

9. I would train my horses and ride them in horse _____.

10. I think _____ I will make a wonderful rancher!

| shows |
| that |
| chance |
| shiny |

Unit 3
Core Skills Phonics, Grade 3

Consonant Digraph Sounds *k* and *sh*

The consonant digraph **ch** usually stands for the sound you hear at the beginning of **chair**. It can also stand for the **k** sound you hear in **orchid** and the **sh** sound you hear in **chef**.

orchid

chef

Find the word at the left that names each picture. Write the word on the line.

chandelier chef chemicals	**1.** 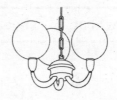_____	**2.** _____	**3.** _____
parachute chemist chorus	**4.** _____	**5.** _____	**6.** _____

Circle the word in each sentence that has a <u>ch</u> digraph. Circle the correct sound for <u>ch</u> at the right.

7. The orchestra played beautiful music.   **k**   **sh**

8. Dave dreams of studying monarch butterflies.   **k**   **sh**

9. Kara sang out in the mountains and heard an echo. **k**   **sh**

10. Ben's uncle has a bushy mustache.   **k**   **sh**

11. Jennifer wants to build big machines when she grows up.   **k**   **sh**

12. The doctor can cure your aches and pains.   **k**   **sh**

Consonant Digraphs *ph* and *gh*

The consonant digraphs **ph** and **gh** can stand for the **f** sound. You can hear the **ph** and **gh** in **phone** and **laugh**.

phone

lau**gh**

Draw a line to match each picture to its name. Circle the two letters that stand for the f sound in each word.

1. photograph

4. rough

2. dolphin

5. elephant

3. cough

6. trophy

Circle the word that completes each sentence. Write the word on the line.

7. In (phonics, phrased) we learn the sounds that letters stand for.

8. I wish this meat was not so (turf, tough).

9. Alex knows all the letters in the Russian (autograph, alphabet).

10. Are ten push-ups (elephant, enough) for your age group? _____

11. I picked up the (phone, fun) and called my friend. _____

12. The third graders are working on (graphs, giraffes). _____

Consonant Digraphs in Context

Circle the word that completes each sentence. Write the word on the line.

1. _____ were the gardens that you dreamed about?

   Wheat   Where   Share

2. The gardens were growing in sunny and _____ spots.

   thread   shaky   shady

3. Everybody had a green _____.

   thumb   thunder   thick

4. A _____ could reach out the window to pick vegetables.

   chew   chef   chop

5. My plants were in the ABC order of the _____.

   photograph   microphone   alphabet

6. My garden made people _____.

   laugh   rough   graph

7. I won a _____ for the funniest garden.

   nephew   gopher   trophy

8. I saw one garden in the _____ of the letter **L**.

   shape   shave   sheep

9. Another garden was planted in the shape of a _____.

   wheel   white   while

10. No _____ or parent was hungry.

    chin   child   chimney

Final Consonant Digraphs

Consonant digraphs come at the end of many words. Some have three letters. You can hear a consonant digraph at the end of **brush** and **match**.

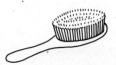

bru**sh**

ma**tch**

Say each picture name. Write the word on the line.

1.

_____

2.

_____

3.

_____

4.

_____

5.

_____

6.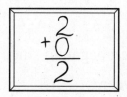

_____

7.

_____

8.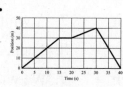

_____

9.

_____

10.

_____

11.

_____

12.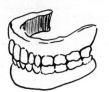

_____

Initial, Medial, and Final Consonant Digraphs in Context

Underline each word that contains the consonant digraph listed at the beginning of the line. Write each underlined word in the correct column.

ng   1. I had always wanted to see the singer named Amelia.

ch   2. My teacher said we would ride on a bus to see her.

th   3. I was third in line.

ph   4. I wanted to get Amelia's autograph.

gh   5. Amelia laughed as she walked onstage.

ch   6. The orchestra began to play.

wh   7. A white light filled the stage.

ch   8. Then, Amelia and a choir of children began to sing.

tch 9. We will watch Amelia again next year.

Beginning	Middle	End
_____	_____	_____
_____	_____	_____
_____	_____	_____
_____	_____	_____

Silent Consonants

Sometimes consonants are **silent**. For example, the **k** in **knot** is silent. The words **wrist**, **comb**, and **light** also have silent consonants.

knot

wrist

com**b**

lig**h**t

Say each picture name. Circle the word that names each picture. Write the word on the line.

1.	knife night knew	2.	wheat wreath wealth	3. 	wrench ranch wreak
4.	fit fight filter	5.	lamb lame limb	6.	key knee lamb
7.	west wrist worst	8.	kite knight nickel	9.	thumb them thirst
10.	comb come column	11.	lit light like	12.	knob nab knock

75

Name _____ Date _____

Silent Consonants in Context

Find the word in the box that completes each sentence. Write the word on the line.

kneels	night
knit	sigh
knot	thumb
lamb	wrap
light	writer

1. I want to be a _____ when I grow up.

2. I write in my journal every _____ before I go to bed.

3. My mom tells me to turn off my _____ when it gets too late.

4. I _____ and ask for five more minutes.

5. Sometimes, I write so long that my _____ gets sore!

6. In my first story, a knight _____ before a king.

7. The king ties a ribbon in a _____ around the knight's sword.

8. I also wrote a story about a _____ that gets lost from its flock.

9. My new story is about a boy who can _____ magic hats.

10. I will _____ the story and give it to my mom.

Syllables

Words are made of small parts called syllables. Each **syllable** has one vowel sound. A word can have one or more syllables.

Find the word in the box that names each picture. Write the word on the line. Then say the word and listen for the number of syllables. Write the word in the correct column below.

| ambulance | desk | hose | volcano | violin | robin | puppet | wagon | pot |

1. _____

2. _____

3. _____

4. _____

5. _____

6. _____

7. _____

8. _____

9. _____

One Syllable	Two Syllables	Three Syllables
_____	_____	_____
_____	_____	_____
_____	_____	_____

Syllables in Context

Use the words in the box to answer the riddles.

banana	boat	cactus	five	kitten
octopus	tiger	umbrella	vest	zipper

1. It rhymes with "nest".
   It's something you can wear.

   It's a _____.

2. It rhymes with "hive".
   It's one more than four.

   It's _____.

3. It rhymes with "goat".
   It travels on water.

   It's a _____.

4. It can be on a jacket.
   It moves up and down.

   It's a _____.

5. It is a desert plant.
   It might stick you.

   It's a _____.

6. It is soft and purrs.
   It's a baby cat.

   It's a _____.

7. It has stripes and roars.
   It's a big cat.

   It's a _____.

8. It has eight arms.
   It lives in the sea.

   It's an _____.

9. It is good to have in the rain.
   It has a handle and opens wide.

   It's an _____.

10. It is a yellow fruit.
    It grows in a bunch.

    It's a _____.

Review Consonant Blends, Digraphs and Syllables

Read each clue. Use a word from the box to complete the answer. Write it on the line.

clock	frog	phone	string	twelve	whale

1. I am the biggest mammal.

I am a _____.

2. I live in a pond.

I am a _____.

3. I am one dozen.

I am _____.

4. I have numbers and I ring.

I am a _____.

5. I have two hands and a face.

I am a _____.

6. I hold a kite.

I am a _____.

Say each picture name. Write the number of syllables in each word on the line.

7.

_____

8.

_____

9.

_____

10.

_____

11.

_____

12.

_____

Review Consonant Blends, Digraphs and Silent Consonants: Scrambled Words

Unscramble the words in the box. Write them on the lines.

scthe	glhit	kwrec
prgnis	wpih	sdtna
arhcn	ucogh	mcbo

Unit 3
Core Skills Phonics, Grade 3

Review Consonant Blends, Digraphs and Silent Consonants in Context

Circle the word that completes each sentence. Write the word on the line.

1. I dreamed of a beach that was pure and (clean, cheek).   _____

2. (Chatter, Children) ran on the white sand.   _____

3. (Dolphins, Drops) swam near the shore.   _____

4. A whale (sprayed, screened) water from its spout.   _____

5. I (played, phoned) in the sand and made a castle.   _____

6. I (wrist, wrote) a message in the sand.   _____

7. It said, "(Thanks, Thinks) for this beautiful day!"   _____

8. Even the seagulls (sang, sank) a special song.   _____

9. It was a great day to (laugh, loud) and play.   _____

10. At (knit, night), the sky was full of stars.   _____

Name _____ Date _____

Reading Comprehension: Consonant Blends, Digraphs and Silent Consonants

Read the letter. Then read the sentences below it. Write the word that completes each sentence.

> March 31, 2014
>
> Dear Ling,
>
> I hope that all of my friends will work together to feed the less fortunate families in our town. I am writing to ask for your help with a special lunch.
>
> On Thursday, a dairy farmer gave cheese. My sister got some fresh mushrooms from the farmers' market. My brother and his friends went to the beach and dug up some clams. I asked my mother to bake something. She agreed to make some wheat bread. On Friday, I phoned three more friends. A man with an orchard gave me twelve bushels of cherries. His friend gave me peach jam. I talked to the manager of our apartment building. She gave us chairs and tables to use for our lunch.
>
> Can you help us, too? I hope so!
>
> Your friend,
> Chad

1. The dairy farmer gave _____ for the meal.

2. Chad's sister got _____ mushrooms from the market.

3. Chad's mother will bake _____ bread.

4. Chad used the _____ to call more friends.

5. The man with the orchard gave _____ bushels of cherries.

Quiz Yourself!

Circle the word that names each picture. Write the word on the line.

1.

scum
screw
skunk

_____

2.

fruit
foot
flute

_____

3.

twist
twig
thirst

_____

4.

wait
whale
water

_____

5.

ship
sheep
sheen

_____

6.

lag
log
laugh

_____

7.

match
march
mash

_____

8.
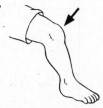
knock
knee
near

_____

9.

nice
knight
night

_____

10.

spirit
spring
string

_____

11.

white
wheat
wheel

_____

12.

bright
branch
brag

_____

Quiz Yourself!, p. 2

Fill in the circle next to the word that completes each sentence. Write the word on the line.

1. I _____ about gardens growing everywhere.
   - ○ cream
   - ○ dream
   - ○ gleam

2. Yellow _____ grows in office windows.
   - ○ squash
   - ○ squish
   - ○ splash

3. A _____ tree grows in every front yard.
   - ○ peach
   - ○ perch
   - ○ beach

4. Everybody has a green _____.
   - ○ them
   - ○ thud
   - ○ thumb

5. Every empty lot is now a field of _____.
   - ○ wheat
   - ○ whole
   - ○ whale

6. People greet each other with a _____.
   - ○ flower
   - ○ flutter
   - ○ flounder

7. A _____ of flowers hangs on every door.
   - ○ wrench
   - ○ wrist
   - ○ wreath

8. Plants grow during all _____ months of the year.
   - ○ shelf
   - ○ twist
   - ○ twelve

9. All the plants get plenty of water and _____.
   - ○ fright
   - ○ flight
   - ○ light

10. I _____ it is a wonderful place.
    - ○ know
    - ○ knit
    - ○ knob

Unit 3 Assessment

Circle the word that names each picture. Write the word on the line.

1.
crown
clock
block

_____

2.
snap
small
shell

_____

3.
shake
whale
whole

_____

4.
swim
slide
star

_____

5.
warm
wasp
walk

_____

6.
tree
creep
try

_____

7.
blink
glove
drove

_____

8.
fun
phone
drove

_____

9.
laugh
fluff
log

_____

10.
neck
never
nest

_____

11.
thumb
trash
test

_____

12.
chaps
chef
cheese

_____

Unit 3 Assessment, p. 2

Fill in the circle next to the word that completes each sentence.

1. The _____ will protect the king.
   - ○ flight
   - ○ knight
   - ○ blight

2. Tie the _____ around the box.
   - ○ string
   - ○ bring
   - ○ straw

3. Please _____ your hair.
   - ○ comb
   - ○ thumb
   - ○ climb

4. What did you _____ for?
   - ○ dish
   - ○ whip
   - ○ wish

5. A plumber uses a _____.
   - ○ wrench
   - ○ wren
   - ○ wrong

6. A _____ blew off that tree.
   - ○ lunch
   - ○ branch
   - ○ launch

7. I am sick with a bad _____.
   - ○ rough
   - ○ cost
   - ○ cough

8. Let's _____ ball after school.
   - ○ play
   - ○ plow
   - ○ plate

9. A _____ fell off the wagon.
   - ○ wheel
   - ○ why
   - ○ whale

10. The _____ is ringing.
    - ○ telephone
    - ○ television
    - ○ telescope

11. Here's a _____ to sweep the floor.
    - ○ stool
    - ○ drum
    - ○ broom

12. She wore her green _____.
    - ○ vent
    - ○ vest
    - ○ best

r-Controlled Vowels *ar* and *or*

When **r** follows a vowel, it changes the vowel sound. You can hear the **ar** sound in **car** and the **or** sound in **corn** and **worm**. The vowel in each is neither long nor short.

car   corn   worm

Find the word in the box that names each picture. Write the word on the line. Circle the letters that stand for the vowel sound you hear in <u>car</u>, <u>corn</u>, or <u>worm</u>.

fork	jar	barn

1.

_____

2.

_____

3.

_____

Find the word in the box that completes each sentence. Write the word on the line.

4. People all around the _____ look at the stars.

5. We can see the stars best after _____.

6. By _____ the stars seem to disappear.

7. Just think how _____ away all those stars are!

8. Look _____, south, east, and west to see stars.

9. Learning about stars is _____ the effort.

dark
far
morning
north
world
worth

r-Controlled Vowels *er, ir,* and *ur*

The letter pairs **er**, **ir**, and **ur** all have the same sound. You can hear this sound in **fern**, **bird**, and **nurse**. The vowel in each is neither short nor long.

fern   **bird**   **nurse**

Circle the word that names each picture. Write the word on the line.

1. porch purse perch	2. skirt shirt skill	3.  turned thirteen turtle
_____	_____	_____
4.  paper person purple	5. cinch circle curdle	6.  girl grill germ
_____	_____	_____

Find the word in the box that completes each sentence. Write the word on the line.

7. The _____ had animals from around the world.

8. We saw ten tiny dogs _____ flips in the air.

9. Three tigers jumped through _____ hoops of fire.

10. A _____ danced on the back of a prancing horse.

11. We were afraid she might get _____.

12. I am _____ that I don't want to try that trick!

burning
certain
circus
girl
hurt
turn

r-Controlled Vowels *air*, *are*, *ear*, and *eer*

The letters **air**, **are**, and **ear** can stand for the same sound. You can hear this sound in **deer**, **chair**, **square**, and **bear**.

deer

chair

square

bear

Say each picture name. Write the letters to complete the word.

1.

   h_____ _____ _____

2.

   p_____ _____ r

3.

   m_____ _____ _____

Find the word in the box that completes each sentence. Write the word on the line.

4. People all over the world have fun at _____.

5. Farmers come to sell _____ and other fruits.

6. Some people _____ their foods and crafts.

7. Dancers often _____ colorful costumes.

8. Sometimes, the dancers put flowers in their _____.

9. They must be careful not to _____ their fancy clothes!

fairs
hair
pears
share
tear
wear

r-Controlled Vowels *ear* and *eer* in Context

The letters **ear** and **eer** can stand for the vowel sound you hear in **beard** and **cheer**. The letters **ear** can also stand for the vowel sound you hear in **Earth**.

beard   cheer   Earth

Read each sentence. Circle each word that contains the vowel sound you hear in <u>beard</u>, <u>cheer</u>, **or** <u>Earth</u>. **Write each word in the correct column below.**

1. All over the world, many people live in or near cities.

2. They peer out their windows at the city streets.

3. Other people live on farms where they plow the earth.

4. They rise early, when they hear the rooster crow.

5. It is hard to earn a living far from a city or a farm.

6. Most people search hard for a good job.

7. Some people must learn new skills for a job.

8. A job that you have for many years is called a career.

ear as in beard	**eer as in cheer**	**ear as in Earth**
_____	_____	_____
_____	_____	_____
_____		_____
		_____
		_____

Name _____   Date _____

Decoding and Syllabicating Words with *r*-Controlled Vowels

> A **syllable** is a word or a word part with one vowel sound. **Rug** has one syllable, **cabin** has two syllables, and **umbrella** has three syllables.

Say each picture name. Find the word in the box that names each picture. Write the word on the line. Then write the number of syllables in each word on the shorter line.

| bear | circus | evergreens | feather | groceries | harbor |

1. _____ ___   2. _____ ___   3. _____ ___

4. _____ ___   5. _____ ___   6. _____ ___

Find the word in the box that completes each sentence. Write the word on the line. Then write the number of syllables in the word on the second line.

| atmosphere   certainly   forests   important |

7. Planting a tree is one of the most _____ ways to   _____
   help our planet.

8. Trees improve the air quality by adding oxygen to the _____.   _____

9. In national _____, trees provide habitats for animals.   _____

10. It is _____ one of the best ways to help Earth.   _____

Decoding and Syllabicating Words with *r*-Controlled Vowels in Context

Circle the word that completes each sentence. Write the word on the line.

1. Nora and her family will never _____ their trip to Ireland.
   forest   forget   furrow

2. They got up _____ one morning to visit Galway Bay.
   early   earnest   eagle

3. They drove through the chilly _____ and clouds of fog.
   ape   art   air

4. It was hard to _____ through the fog.
   pear   peer   pair

5. Then the fog lifted, and they got a _____ view of the bay.
   clear   cheer   chorus

6. "Ireland is the most beautiful place in the _____!" shouted Nora.
   world   work   worth

7. Nora's family visited an Irish _____.
   form   firm   farm

8. Nora's brother _____ her to pet a sheep.
   dreary   dared   darken

9. The farmer let her touch its _____ wool.
   cured   curb   curly

10. Nora's family bought wool sweaters to _____.
    wear   wore   were

Unit 4
Core Skills Phonics, Grade 3

y as a Vowel

The letter **y** can act as a vowel. You can hear the **long i** sound of y in **fly**, the **long e** sound of y in **baby**, and the **short i** sound of y in **gym**.

fly

baby

gym

Find the word in the box that names each picture. Write the word on the line. Write the word in the correct column below.

| bicycle | cherry | cry | cymbals | fry | funny | penny | pyramid | sky |

1. _____

2. _____

3. _____

4. _____

5. _____

6. _____

7. _____

8. _____

9. _____

y as long i

_____

_____

_____

y as long e

_____

_____

_____

y as short i

_____

_____

_____

93

y as a Vowel and Syllables in Context

> When a word with one syllable ends in **y**, the **y** usually has the **long i** sound.
>
> When a word with two or more syllables ends in **y**, the **y** usually has the **long e** sound.
>
> When **y** comes in the middle of a word or a syllable, it usually has the **short i** sound.

Say each word in the box. Write the word in the correct column below.

cry	fry	history	mystery	rainy	shy	sunny	syllable	system

One Syllable	Two Syllables	Three Syllables
_____	_____	_____
_____	_____	_____

Say each word below. Write the number of syllables you hear on the line. Find the word in the box that completes each sentence. Write the word on the line.

dry _____	Egypt _____	mystery _____
pyramid _____	royalty _____	why _____

1. A _____ is a large building with sides shaped like triangles.

2. Many were built long ago in the country of _____.

3. You can find them there in the hot, _____ desert.

4. Experts know _____ they were built.

5. They were built as a place to bury kings and other _____.

6. How they were built is still a _____.

Schwa

The **schwa** is the vowel sound you hear in an unstressed syllable. Any vowel can stand for the schwa sound. You can hear the schwa sound in **asleep**, **melon**, **pencil**, **circus**, and **elephant**.

   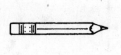 

asleep   mel**o**n   penc**i**l   circ**u**s   eleph**a**nt

The words at the left name the pictures in each row. Write each word under its picture. Circle the vowel that stands for the schwa sound.

seven walrus zebra	1. 2. 3.
gerbil wagon telephone	4. 5. 6.
cactus apricots parrot	7. 8. 9.
camel canoe president	10. 11. 12.

Unit 4
Core Skills Phonics, Grade 3

Schwa in Context

Find the word in the box that completes each sentence. Write the word on the line.

album	alone
carrots	eleven
lemons	possible
presents	science
shovel	problems

1. Cyrus only has _____ cents in his bank.

2. He wants to give his family some _____.

3. Cyrus knows that it is _____ to give presents that don't cost money.

4. He can help his sister study for her _____ test.

5. Cyrus can help his brother solve his math _____.

6. Cyrus can squeeze _____ to make his dad's favorite drink.

7. He can help his mom peel _____ and potatoes for dinner.

8. He can visit his grandmother, who lives all _____.

9. Next winter, he can help _____ the snow.

10. Cyrus can make a photo _____ for his family.

Review *r*-Controlled Vowels, *y* as a Vowel, and Schwa

Find the word in the box that names each picture. Write the word on the line.

| girl | chair | rainy | baby | lion | pearl |
| panda | cherry | octopus | barber | flower | fly |

1.

_____

2.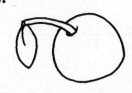

_____

3.

_____

4.

_____

5.

_____

6.

_____

7.

_____

8.

_____

9.

_____

10.

_____

11.

_____

12.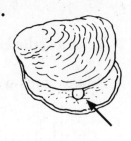

_____

Review *r*-Controlled Vowels, *y* as a Vowel, and Schwa: Secret Code

Use the code to write each missing word.

1 = a	2 = b	3 = c	4 = d	5 = e	6 = h
7 = i	8 = l	9 = m	10 = n	11 = o	12 = p
13 = r	14 = s	15 = t	16 = w	17 = y	

1. Sailors long ago traveled all over the ____ ____ ____ ____ ____ .
   16   11   13   8   4

2. Some sailors told stories about ____ ____ ____ ____ ____ ____ ____ ____ .
   9   5   13   9   1   7   4   14

3. Some sailors lost their ships to ____ ____ ____ ____ ____ ____ ____ .
   12   7   13   1   15   5   14

4. Most sailors were not ____ ____ ____ about telling their stories.
   14   6   17

5. Some sailors dove to ____ ____ ____ ____ ____ ____
   14   5   1   13   3   6

   for ____ ____ ____ ____ ____ ____ .
   12   5   1   13   8   14

6. A ____ ____ ____ ____ ____ ____ ____ ____ ____ ____ could
   16   7   10   4   17   14   15   11   13   9

   send a sailor's ship off course.

7. Many ships were lost every ____ ____ ____ ____ .
   17   5   1   13

8. The wind could ____ ____ ____ ____ a ship's sails.
   15   5   1   13

9. A lighthouse helped during the ____ ____ ____ ____ ____ storms.
   16   11   13   14   15

10. The ____ ____ ____ ____ ____ of a foghorn helped, too.
    2   8   1   13   5

Review *r*-Controlled Vowels, *y* as a Vowel, and Schwa in Context

Complete each sentence with a word from the box. Write the word on the line.

adult	canoe
dirt	experts
furry	perch
squirrels	surprised
under	were
world	worms

1. What kind of wildlife is right _____ your feet?

2. You might be _____ by what you can find.

3. You might see a _____ raccoon bustle by with food.

4. Perhaps you'll watch a bird fly from its _____ high in a tree.

5. You can see _____ run along the ground gathering nuts.

6. Maybe an _____ will take you fishing.

7. You can ride in a _____ downstream.

8. You'll find a whole new _____ underground.

9. Dig carefully into the grass and _____.

10. You'll find more than just _____ inching around.

11. _____ have told us that many tiny animals live underground.

12. Let us know if they _____ right!

Reading Comprehension: *r*-Controlled Vowels, *y* as a Vowel, and Schwa

Read the passage. Then read the sentences below it. Write the word that completes each sentence.

Mount Everest

Mount Everest is the highest mountain on Earth. It is more than 29,000 feet tall. It is in the mountain range called the Himalayas. People who live in this mountain range call it the Roof of the World.

Mountain climbers first reached the top of Mount Everest in 1953. Only two people made it to the top that year. In later years, thousands climbed to the top. Many of them left their garbage behind. The Roof of the World was littered with tons of garbage. The problem became an emergency.

In 1994, five American climbers went up the mountain. They brought back more than 5,000 pounds of ripped-up tents and camping gear, batteries, and other garbage. They also paid Sherpas to carry garbage down Mount Everest. The Sherpas are the people who live near the mountain.

Today, cleanup crews search for the worst dumps. They hope that future climbers will carry their own garbage down the mountain. They want the Roof of the World to be clean again.

1. Mount Everest is _____ than 29,000 feet tall.

2. People first stood at the top of Mount Everest in the _____ 1953.

3. Many climbers left old tents and other _____ on the mountain.

4. The garbage problem became an _____.

5. Cleanup crews try to find the _____ dumps to clean.

Vowel Digraphs *ea* and *ei*

A **vowel digraph** is two vowels that are together. Vowel digraphs can have a short vowel sound, a long vowel sound, or a sound all their own.
The vowel digraph **ea** can stand for the **short e** sound you hear in **bread**.
The vowel digraph **ei** can stand for the **long a** sound you hear in **sleigh**.

bread   sleigh

Say each picture name. Write __ea__ or __ei__ on the line to complete the word.

1.  r_____n	2. h____d	3.  v_____l	4. sw_____ter
5. 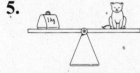 w_____gh	6. p_____r	7. w_____ght	8. tr____d
9. n_____ghbors	10. f_____ther	11. 8 _____ght	12. thr_____d

Vowel Digraphs *ea* and *ei* in Context

Read the story. Underline each word that has the <u>short e</u> sound of <u>ea</u>. Circle each word that has the <u>long a</u> sound of <u>ei</u>.

Emma and her neighbor Hans live in Germany. After breakfast one day, they rode horses in the hills outside Munich. Emma's horse didn't like the weight of the saddle on its back.

"That saddle is very heavy," Hans said.

Emma held the leather reins and patted the horse gently. They rode until they saw a meadow on the hillside ahead.

"This is heavenly," said Hans. "Look at all these flowers. Daisies and heather are spread out as far as I can see."

"The weather is nice, too," Emma said. She slid off her horse and tied her sweater around her waist.

Emma's horse neighed once and lowered its head. It began to eat the grass. They were all ready to take a pleasant break from riding.

Circle the word that completes each sentence. Write the word on the line.

1. Emma and Hans are _____.

   reindeer   neighbors   treasures

2. Emma's horse had a _____ saddle.

   sweaty   heavy   eighty

3. The horse didn't like the _____ of the saddle.

   weight   eighteen   vein

4. Emma and Hans stopped in a _____ full of flowers.

   breakfast   measure   meadow

5. There were daisies and _____ on the hillside.

   heaven   heather   sweater

Vowel Digraph *oo*

The vowel digraph **oo** can stand for the vowel sounds you hear in **book** and **moon**.

book

moon

Circle the word that names each picture. Write the word on the line.

1.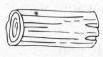
   would
   wood
   word

   _____

2.
   roof
   ruff
   root

   _____

3.
   hoop
   honk
   hook

   _____

4.
   wool
   work
   wall

   _____

5.
   racing
   racket
   raccoon

   _____

6.
   school
   scold
   should

   _____

7.
   book
   bore
   boot

   _____

8.
   pool
   pour
   pop

   _____

9.
   kangaroo
   kettle
   kitchen

   _____

10.
    ballet
    baboon
    balloon

    _____

11.
    food
    foot
    fork

    _____

12.
    sport
    spot
    spoon

    _____

103

Vowel Digraph *oo* in Context

Read the story. Circle each word that has the <u>oo</u> digraph. Write each word in the correct column below.

The Paynes raise sheep in New Zealand. Wool is an important product in their country. The Paynes didn't learn their skills in school. It took a long time to learn how to raise the best sheep.

The Paynes look over their flock carefully. They feed the sheep the best food and check their health often. They guide the sheep to pasture with big canes made of bamboo.

One cool spring night, Nate Payne was in his room. He heard a ewe, a female sheep, crying. Nate stood up and put on his boots. He went out to find the ewe. He saw her standing in the moonlight. She was caught in a hawthorn bush. Her foot was stuck in the branches. Her curly hair was tangled in the thorns.

"Goodness!" Nate said as he kneeled down to help her. "You have really cooked your goose!" He carefully unhooked the thorns from the ewe's thick fur.

oo as in book		**oo as in moon**	
_____	_____	_____	_____
_____	_____	_____	_____
_____	_____	_____	_____

Vowel Digraphs *ew* and *ui*

> The vowel digraphs **ew** and **ui** can stand for the same vowel sound. You can hear this vowel sound in **screw** and **fruit**.
>
>
>
> screw   fr**ui**t

Circle the word that names each picture. Write the word on the line.

1.	jester jewel jelly	2.	suit soup soon	3.	needle newspaper noontime
_____		_____		_____	
4. 	stem straw stew	5.	chew choose cherry	6.	junk judge juice
_____		_____		_____	

Find the word in the box that completes each sentence. Write the word on the line.

7. The Chen family went on a _____ to the South Pacific.

8. The Chens visited quite a _____ beautiful islands.

9. A soft, warm breeze _____ through the palm trees.

10. Colorful birds _____ all around and perched nearby.

11. Mrs. Chen fed them little pieces of _____ .

12. The birds loved the _____ treat!

blew
cruise
few
flew
fruit
juicy

105

Vowel Digraphs *ew* and *ui* in Context

Circle the word that completes each sentence.
Write the word on the line.

1. Maria reads the paper every day to keep up with the _____.

   nose   news   noose

2. Yesterday, Maria read about a frost that hurt the _____ trees in Florida.

   root   fruit   friend

3. The morning _____ froze on the plants.

   due   dew   do

4. Some oranges were _____ when they fell to the ground.

   brushed   bruised   brood

5. Maria thinks that the price of _____ will go up soon.

   juice   joyous   jelly

6. Then Maria read about a famous artist that her mother _____.

   knee   kneel   knew

7. The artist sailed around the world to find the best _____.

   vow   view   vowel

8. She _____ pictures of the places she liked most.

   drew   drain   dregs

9. She painted sea gulls that _____ over England's cliffs.

   flea   few   flew

10. She painted the ocean as the wind _____ over the waves.

    blue   blew   blend

Vowel Digraphs *au, aw,* and *al*

The vowel digraphs **au** and **aw** can stand for the same vowel sound. You can hear this vowel sound in **haul** and **paw**.

The letters **al** can stand for this same vowel sound. You can hear this sound in **chalk** and **ball**.

haul   paw   chalk   ball

Say each picture name. Write <u>au</u>, <u>aw</u>, or <u>al</u> on the line to complete the word.

1.  f____l	2. y____n	3. w____k	4. v____lt
5.  s____	6.  f____cet	7.  l____n	8. w____l
9.  s____cer	10.  cr____l	11. astron____t	12. h____k

107

Vowel Digraphs *au*, *aw*, and *al* in Context

Find the word in the box that completes each sentence. Write the word on the line.

always	autumn	call	crawl	dawn
launch	salty	sauce	saw	shawl

1. I have _____ liked to learn about other places.

2. When it is _____ in South America, it is spring in Canada.

3. When the sun sets in Brazil, it is _____ in Australia.

4. I wonder how much a phone _____ to Spain costs.

5. All kinds of insects fly and _____ through the rain forest.

6. The Great Salt Lake in Utah has _____ water.

7. I watched a rocket _____ in Florida.

8. My grandmother bought a beautiful knitted _____ in Russia.

9. My uncle learned to make spicy tomato _____ in Italy.

10. My mom went to Paris and _____ the Eiffel Tower.

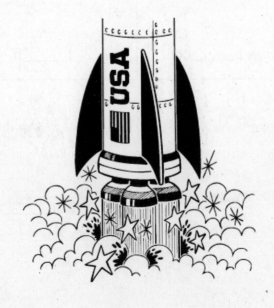

Vowel Digraph and Diphthong *ou*

A **diphthong** is two vowels blended together to make one vowel sound.
The diphthong **ou** can stand for the vowel sound you hear in **mouse**.

mouse

**Say each picture name. If the word has the same vowel sound that you hear in mouse,
write the diphthong ou to complete the word.**

1. c_____ch	2. h_____se	3. r_____gh	4. d_____r
5. sp_____t	6. fl_____r	7. m_____th	8. t_____d
9. cl_____d	10. c_____gar	11. g_____rd	12. bl_____se

Core Skills Phonics, Grade 3

Vowel Digraph and Diphthong *ou* in Context

Find the word in the box that completes each sentence. Use each word only once.
Write the word on the line.

brought	countries	course	enough	gourds
group	rough	tough	trouble	you

1. The Pilgrims came to New England from _____ in Europe.

2. They sailed across the ocean on _____ waters.

3. They had a _____ time settling in America.

4. They had _____ growing food.

5. The Native Americans _____ food to the Pilgrims through the winter.

6. The Pilgrims learned how to grow pumpkins and _____.

7. Soon, there was _____ food to keep the Pilgrims alive.

8. The whole _____ was happy with this new friendship.

9. Would _____ be helpful to a new friend?

10. Of _____ you would!

Diphthongs *ow, oy,* and *oi*

> The diphthong **ow** can stand for the sound you hear in **cow**.
> It can also stand for the **long o** sound you hear in **crow**.

cow   crow

The words at the left name the pictures in each row. Write each word under its picture.

toys soil point	1.  _____	2. _____	3. _____
coil broil noise	4. _____	5. _____	6. _____
boil oyster foil	7. _____	8. _____	9. _____
crown snow flower	10. _____	11. _____	12. _____

Diphthongs *ow*, *oy*, and *oi* in Context

Find the word in the box that completes each sentence. Write the word on the line.

annoy	enjoy	glow	how	join
oil	owl	snow	tower	voyage

1. Would you _____ exploring the arctic?

2. It is not easy to _____ a team of explorers.

3. You would have to be strong enough for the _____.

4. You would have to learn to live in the _____.

5. Good explorers do not let the cold weather _____ them.

6. Explorers once used _____ lanterns.

7. The _____ of your lantern would last all night.

8. You might see an _____ looking for food.

9. You would have to learn _____ to live without television.

10. There's no TV _____ at the North Pole!

Review Vowel Digraphs and Diphthongs

Find the word in the box that names each picture. Write the word on the line.

| book | cough | Earth | fruit | hawk | jewel |
| mouse | news | owl | soup | spoon | toys |

1.

_____

2.

_____

3.

_____

4.

_____

5.

_____

6.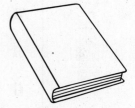

_____

7.

_____

8.

_____

9.

_____

10.

_____

11.

_____

12.

_____

Review Vowel Digraphs and Diphthongs: Word Find

Find and circle the words from the box in the puzzle below. The words can go across or down.

```
v  a  u  l  t  m  a  l  l  x
o  a  w  e  s  p  o  o  n  n
w  j  o  y  a  l  l  c  e  e
b  e  c  a  u  s  e  n  i  w
o  w  r  w  c  p  a  o  g  s
u  e  e  n  e  r  a  i  h  p
n  l  w  k  a  e  n  s  b  a
d  t  o  u  r  a  n  e  o  p
b  o  o  k  t  d  o  a  r  e
t  o  u  g  h  k  y  o  u  r
```

annoy	neighbor
awe	newspaper
book	noise
bound	spoon
cause	spread
crew	tough
earth	tour
jewel	vault
joy	yawn
mall	your

Unit 4
Core Skills Phonics, Grade 3

Review Vowel Digraphs and Diphthongs in Context

Read each sentence. Replace <u>suitcase</u> **with the correct word from the box. Write the word on the line at the bottom of the page.**

1. Have you ever **suitcase** about living in another country?

2. In Peru, you could watch **suitcase** fly high in the sky.

3. In Italy, cooks add tomato **suitcase** to many foods.

4. You would need big scales to **suitcase** an Indian elephant.

5. You can see rain **suitcase** down in the rain forest.

6. Would you like to fish in a **suitcase** in Sweden?

7. The howler monkeys in South America are **suitcase**.

8. I like to travel **suitcase** the world.

9. But I am **suitcase** every time I come home.

10. Home is **suitcase** the best place to be.

| always |
| around |
| brook |
| hawks |
| joyful |
| noisy |
| pour |
| sauce |
| thought |
| weigh |

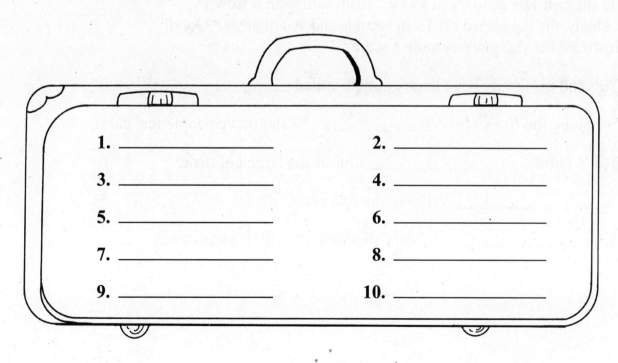

1. _____ 2. _____

3. _____ 4. _____

5. _____ 6. _____

7. _____ 8. _____

9. _____ 10. _____

Reading Comprehension: Vowel Digraphs and Diphthongs

Read the story. Then read the sentences below it. Write the word that completes each sentence.

A Koi Story

Some fish farmers in Japan raise large goldfish called koi. These fish come in many colors. People like to watch koi swim around. Watching them helps people feel calm and relaxed.

A boy named Yuji talked his parents into getting a few koi. They bought four fish and put them in a pond near the house. They fed the koi special food. The fish seemed to enjoy their new home well enough. Soon there were fourteen of them.

One day, Yuji was playing baseball in the yard with a couple of friends. Just as he threw the ball, he tripped over a coiled hose. The ball went into the pond. Most of the koi swam down and away, but one jumped out of the pool.

"Quick!" Yuji shouted loudly. "Throw it back in! It can't breathe air!"

His friend Toshi picked up the fish and lowered it into the water. It didn't move. It looked more brown than gold. Toshi thought the fish was dead. "I'm sorry," Toshi said with a frown.

Suddenly, the koi leaped off Toshi's hands and swam away. "Good!" said Toshi. "That fish gave us quite a scare."

1. Yuji and his family have large goldfish called _____.

2. Watching the fish swim _____ can make people feel calm.

3. Yuji's family _____ four of the large goldfish.

4. A _____ fell into the fish pond.

5. Toshi _____ the fish was dead until it swam away.

Name _____ Date _____

Quiz Yourself!

Circle the word that names each picture. Write the word on the line.

1.
worm
warm
work

_____

2.
cool
cold
coil

_____

3.
turtle
turkey
turned

_____

4.
old
ouch
owl

_____

5.
stores
stairs
stares

_____

6.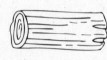
wood
wool
would

_____

7.
pawn
paw
park

_____

8.
dear
deer
dreary

_____

9.
shout
sprout
spout

_____

10.
star
stall
start

_____

11.
beard
break
bread

_____

12.
jet
jewel
jester

_____

Unit 4
Core Skills Phonics, Grade 3

Quiz Yourself!, p. 2

Fill in the circle next to the word that completes each sentence. Write the word on the line.

1. One day, I will take a _____ around the world.
   - ○ vowel   ○ voices
   - ○ voyage

2. I will travel at least _____ months.
   - ○ four   ○ fork
   - ○ form

3. The rain _____ is home to many important plants and animals.
   - ○ forty   ○ forest
   - ○ force

4. My teacher went to Tanzania and saw a _____ of zebra.
   - ○ horse   ○ heard
   - ○ herd

5. There are _____ on every continent on Earth.
   - ○ mother   ○ mouthy
   - ○ mountains

6. I like to _____ downtown in the cities I visit.
   - ○ wall   ○ walk
   - ○ wail

7. The _____ in Egypt were built as tombs for kings.
   - ○ parachutes   ○ pyramids
   - ○ palaces

8. Would you like to take a _____ to Greece?
   - ○ cruise   ○ crews
   - ○ clues

9. I will _____ like to travel.
   - ○ already   ○ always
   - ○ weigh

10. Don't be _____ to try new things.
    - ○ scared   ○ scarf
    - ○ scarred

118

Unit 4 Assessment

Circle the word that names each picture. Write the word on the line.

1.

crowd
cloud
clown

_____

2.

brain
brag
braid

_____

3.

dear
tear
deer

_____

4.

course
coins
cruise

_____

5.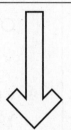

door
dock
down

_____

6.

suit
sew
soon

_____

7.

broom
bread
break

_____

8.

walk
what
wall

_____

9.

clown
clock
down

_____

10.

bread
bear
beard

_____

11.

carp
card
cart

_____

12.

new
newt
noon

_____

Unit 4 Assessment, p. 2

Fill in the circle next to the word that completes each sentence.

1. My favorite color is _____.
   - ○ people
   - ○ purple
   - ○ purse

2. Mr. Goldman has a bushy _____.
   - ○ barn
   - ○ book
   - ○ beard

3. Jenny is sick with a bad _____.
   - ○ catch
   - ○ caught
   - ○ cough

4. A small _____ hid under our couch.
   - ○ moo
   - ○ mouse
   - ○ must

5. The _____ cut my hair while I sat in the chair.
   - ○ barber
   - ○ bargain
   - ○ border

6. Yesterday was a cold and _____ day.
   - ○ dared
   - ○ dreary
   - ○ dairy

7. How much does a baby elephant _____?
   - ○ weather
   - ○ world
   - ○ weigh

8. You _____ just like your mother.
   - ○ look
   - ○ loud
   - ○ lawn

9. Close your mouth when you _____ your food.
   - ○ crow
   - ○ course
   - ○ chew

10. My favorite _____ is the rose.
    - ○ foil
    - ○ flower
    - ○ fought

11. Dad dried the cups and _____ with a dish towel.
    - ○ saucers
    - ○ seesaw
    - ○ sausage

12. The _____ flew back to her nest.
    - ○ cow
    - ○ crow
    - ○ cheer

Answer Key

Page 1
1. *b*   5. rug   9. laugh
2. *x*   6. sun   10. coins
3. *f*   7. tree   11. clown
4. mop   8. glove   12. deer

Page 2
1. cap
2. goats
3. banana
4. bat
5. lake
6. pine
7. cough
8. broom
9. comb
10. look
11. saucers
12. beard

Page 3
1. *b*   4. *s*   7. *r*   10. *p*
2. *z*   5. *d*   8. *m*   11. *h*
3. *t*   6. *f*   9. *l*   12. *w*

Page 4
1. park   5. nuts   9. young
2. week   6. turtle   10. quiet
3. jeep   7. bird
4. deer   8. fish

Page 5
1. *s*   4. *b*   7. *m*   10. *f*
2. *r*   5. *d*   8. *n*   11. *l*
3. *p*   6. *g*   9. *g*   12. *x*

Page 6
1. work   5. dig   9. grass
2. car   6. hat   10. dam
3. road   7. pencil
4. music   8. box

Page 7
1. *m*   4. *g*   7. *g*   10. *b*
2. *z*   5. *p*   8. *b*   11. *p*
3. *l*   6. *r*   9. *v*   12. *m*

Page 8
1. honey   6. carrot
2. water   7. Bacon
3. lemon   8. butter
4. melon   9. cider
5. muffin   10. sugar

Page 9
1. *s*   4. *v*   7. *m*   10. *c*
2. *k*   5. *rr*   8. *w*   11. *k*
3. *t*   6. *g*   9. *b*   12. *s*

Page 10
1. cabin   5. sofa   9. roof
2. water   6. mug   10. quiet
3. tulip   7. deer
4. lemon   8. fish

Page 11
The following words should be circled:
1. city, country
2. center
3. nice, ice
4. can, taxicab, corner
5. actors
6. : place
soft *c*: city, center, nice, ice, place
hard *c*: country, can, taxicab, corner, actors

Page 12
1. cent   5. pencil   9. cob
2. cub   6. voice   10. fence
3. coat   7. cider
4. cat   8. Call

Page 13
1. tiger   6. igloo
2. gem   7. pigeon
3. dog   8. mug
4. guitar   9. gerbil
5. flag

Page 14
1. gym   6. huge
2. game   7. gold
3. giraffe   8. sugar
4. giant   9. pigeon
5. gentle   10. cage

Page 15
First line: *sh*
Second line: *s*
Third line: *z*
The following words should be circled:
1. tissue
2. sure
3. serve, soup, salad
4. Sandy, is, sick, outside
5. Use, nose, rose
6. likes, peas, beans, fries
sh sound of *s*: tissue, sure
s sound of *s*: serve, soup, salad, Sandy, sick, outside, likes
z sound of *s*: Use, nose, rose, peas, beans, fries
7. sandwich
8. cheese
9. supper
10. sure

Page 16
The following words should be circled:
1. assured, has, books
2. space, mission
3. used, tissue, sad
4. books, music
5. was, sure, leaves
6. as, present
s sound of *s*: books, space, sad, books

z sound of *s*: has, used, music, was, leaves, as, present
sh sound of *s*: assured, mission, tissue, sure

Page 17
1. *c*   6. *s*   11. seven
2. *g*   7. *s*   12. car
3. *s*   8. *s*   13. leaves
4. *g*   9. *ss*   14. igloo
5. *c*   10. camel

Page 18

Color red: ice, center, color, dance
Color blue: gorilla, giraffe, goat, gem
Color green: baseball, rose, sure, solve, sink, museum, dinosaur

Page 19
The following words should be circled:
1. curl
2. big, cat, ice
3. gentle, giant, golf
4. certain
hard *c*: curl, cat
soft *c*: ice, certain
hard *g*: big, golf
soft *g*: gentle, giant
5. bus   8. walrus
6. lessons   9. grill
7. tiger   10. corn

Page 20
1. rodents   4. active
2. gerbil   5. cool
3. hide or sleep

Page 21
1. *x*   4. *t*   7. *c*   10. *g*
2. *t*   5. *g*   8. *b*   11. *s*
3. *m*   6. *m*   9. *f*   12. *c*

Page 22
1. butter   5. mug   9. water
2. gold   6. rise   10. cent
3. sure   7. page
4. books   8. cabin

Page 23
1. *m*   4. *b*   7. *c*   10. *m*
2. *c*   5. *g*   8. *x*   11. *f*
3. *l*   6. *r*   9. *p*   12. *d*

Page 24
1. tissue
2. book
3. giant
4. cap
5. seals
6. feed
7. cabin
8. roses
9. goats
10. circus
11. pot
12. banana

Page 25
Students write **a** under these pictures:
1. bag   6. pan   9. gas
2. dad   7. dam   10. can
4. cat   8. fan

Page 26
1. camp   5. gas   9. at
2. pack   6. map   10. has
3. bag   7. and
4. van   8. pass

Page 27
1. rod   5. pot   9. sock
2. jog   6. dog   10. clock
3. cot   7. cob   11. mop
4. lock   8. top   12. hog

Page 28
Students should underline the following words and write them on the line:
1. Hop   6. Logs
2. Dogs   7. Fox
3. Hot   8. Ponds
4. Pods   9. Hogs
5. Spots   10. Clocks

Page 29
1. lip   5. wig   9. ship
2. knit   6. fish   10. dish
3. bib   7. six   11. hill
4. dig   8. zip   12. stick or twig

Page 30
Order of answers may vary.
1. it's
2. fish
3. give
4. little
5. swish
6. swim
7. with
8. fins
9. dip
10. quickly
11. zip
12. wish
13. flip
14. ship
15. dish
16. fish

Answer Key
Core Skills Phonics, Grade 3

Page 31
Students write **u** under these pictures:
1. bud
6. jug
10. bug
2. cub
7. hug
11. rugs
5. run
9. pup
12. luck

Page 32
1. bus
5. brush
9. bug
2. duck
6. trunk
10. run
3. sun
7. buzz
4. cub
8. tub

Page 33
1. vest
5. bell
10. sled
2. net
6. pen
12. tent
3. ten
7. hen
4. peg
8. egg

Page 34
1. pet, went, set
2. get, eggs, fed
3. well, when, yell
4. help, step, end

Page 35
1. hen
5. rod
9. skunk
2. vest
6. cat
10. ham
3. sun
7. sock
11. bat
4. six
8. egg
12. bug

Page 36
Words should be written in the following order, clockwise or counterclockwise, around the wheel:
cot   pig   jog   bag
pot   dig   jug   bat
pit   dog   bug

Page 37
1. camp
5. sack
9. net
2. fun
6. step
10. ham
3. sun
7. hop
11. swim
4. fan
8. hit
12. cot

Page 38
1. kept
3. added
5. top
2. gas
4. drugstores

Page 39
Students complete the word under these pictures:
1. mail
5. lake
9. ray
2. cane
6. pail
11. bait
3. pay
8. rain
12. sail

Page 40
1. hay
5. paint
9. clay
2. jay
6. snails
10. rays
3. lake
7. cane
4. cake
8. mane

Page 41
1. nose
5. toast
9. boat
2. soap
6. rope
10. row
3. crow
7. toe
11. goal
4. mow
8. dome
12. toad

Page 42
1. show, toast
2. loaned, bow
3. rode, home
4. toad, mole
5. toes, note
6. rose, low, note
7. joke, throat
8. so, glowed

Page 43
1. pipe
4. night
7. vine
2. pie
5. bike
8. smile
3. hike
6. die
9. tie

Page 44
1. dime
5. tight
9. lime
2. night
6. sigh
10. ice
3. right
7. pie
4. mice
8. prize

Page 45
Students complete the word under these pictures:
1. tube
5. ruler
10. flute
2. tune
7. mule
12. fuse
4. plume
9. glue

Page 46
1. Luke
5. cube
9. mule
2. clue
6. blue
10. June
3. use
7. glue
4. huge
8. cute

Page 47
1. team
5. peach
9. queen
2. seed
6. meat
10. feet
3. peas
7. bean
11. seal
4. knee
8. weed
12. leaf

Page 48
1. Lee, see
2. meet, street
3. neat, jeep
4. bee, tree
5. cheep, peep
6. eat, meal
7. sweet, treat
8. sees, Neal
9. need, feed
10. meet, week

Page 49
1. glue
5. tape
9. nail
2. wheel
6. hose
10. bee
3. dune
7. flute
11. toad
4. beak
8. bike
12. nine

Page 50
Students should circle the following words in each grid:
1. game, nail, name
2. tree, bean, bee
3. blue, tune, cube
4. cold, roll, goat
5. hide, light, bite
6. post, hold, dome

Page 51
1. kite
2. bone
3. tube
4. blue
5. queen
6. midnight
7. lime
8. jay
9. tow
10. pane
11. tie
12. jeep

Page 52
1. rules
3. range
5. child
2. three
4. green

Page 53
1. cane
5. hut
9. bike
2. child
6. bed
10. nail
3. map
7. coat
11. duck
4. top
8. bolt
12. van

Page 54
1. cute
5. hike
9. lock
2. pet
6. miss
10. hoe
3. tail
7. team
4. gold
8. cap

Page 55
1. meat
5. vest
9. rug
2. sun
6. fan
10. jay
3. toast
7. nail
11. glue
4. bee
8. mop
12. team

Page 56
1. pay
5. hit
9. sun
2. lost
6. fold
10. bed
3. pine
7. bat
11. lake
4. deep
8. use
12. pack

Page 57
1. skunk; circle: *sk*
2. squeeze; circle: *squ*
3. swim; circle: *sw*
4. smile; circle: *sm*
5. snake; circle: *sn*
6. spill; circle: *sp*
7. stove; circle: *st*
8. star; circle: *st*
9. squash; circle: *squ*
10. snail; circle: *sn*
11. smoke; circle: *sm*
12. spot; circle: *sp*

Page 58
1. scream
2. spray
3. straw
4. screw
5. spring
6. strong
7. stream
8. stretch
9. stray
10. scratch
11. splash
12. stripe

Page 59
1. *br*
4. *pr*
7. *tr*
10. *fr*
2. *cr*
5. *gr*
8. *gr*
11. *tr*
3. *dr*
6. *pr*
9. *br*
12. *dr*

Page 60
s Blends: special, spring, Spain, smiles, snacked, smelled, spaghetti, stay
r Blends: dreamed, trip, grandmother, traveled, greeted, train, grapes, breeze

Page 61
1. clock; circle: *cl*
2. glue; circle: *gl*
3. twins; circle: *tw*
4. twenty; circle: *tw*
5. globe; circle: *gl*
6. flower; circle: *fl*
7. glass; circle: *gl*
8. plum; circle: *pl*
9. plate; circle: *pl*
10. twig; circle: *tw*
11. slide; circle: *sl*
12. cloud; circle: *cl*

Page 62
1. flakes
6. twice
2. clouds
7. plane
3. gloves
8. twelve
4. blue
9. glad
5. sled
10. play

Page 63
1. band
4. nest
7. cent
2. tent
5. lamp
8. wasp
3. vest
6. mask

Page 64
1. list
5. scent
9. hand
2. band
6. camp
10. best
3. vest
7. west
4. belt
8. ask

Page 65
1. *nt*
5. *gr*
9. *rd*
2. *bl*
6. *sl* or *tr*
10. *cr*
3. *nd*
7. *sn*
11. *ng*
4. *sc*
8. *spr*
12. *squ*

Page 67
1. stain
6. thrill
2. cried
7. flock
3. shone
8. sink
4. blame
9. stream
5. lamp
10. dress

Page 68
1. twigs
3. grass
5. great
2. spring
4. frost

Page 69
1. cheek; circle: *ch*
2. thirteen; circle: *th*
3. ship; circle: *sh*
4. wheat; circle: *wh*
5. wheel; circle: *wh*
6. sheep; circle: *sh*
7. chance

Answer Key
Core Skills Phonics, Grade 3

8. shiny
9. shows
10. that

Page 70
1. chemicals
2. chandelier
3. chef
4. chorus
5. chemist
6. parachute
7. Circle: orchestra, *k*
8. Circle: monarch, *k*
9. Circle: echo, *k*
10. Circle: mustache, *sh*
11. Circle: machines, *sh*
12. Circle: aches, *k*

Page 71
Check that students have matched pictures to words.
1. photograph; circle: *ph, ph*
2. dolphin; circle: *ph*
3. cough; circle: *gh*
4. rough; circle: *gh*
5. elephant; circle: *ph*
6. trophy; circle: *ph*
7. phonics
8. tough
9. alphabet
10. enough
11. phone
12. graphs

Page 72
1. Where
2. shady
3. thumb
4. chef
5. alphabet
6. laugh
7. trophy
8. shape
9. wheel
10. child

Page 73
1. peach
2. chick
3. branch
4. clock
5. wing
6. math
7. watch
8. graph
9. fish
10. trash
11. king
12. teeth

Page 74
Students should underline the following words:
1. singer
2. teacher
3. third
4. autograph
5. laughed
6. orchestra
7. white
8. choir, children
9. watch
Beginning: third, white, choir, children
Middle: singer, teacher, laughed, orchestra
End: autograph, watch

Page 75
1. knife
2. wreath
3. wrench
4. fight
5. lamb
6. knee
7. wrist
8. knight
9. thumb
10. comb
11. light
12. knob

Page 76
1. writer
2. night
3. light
4. sigh
5. thumb
6. kneels
7. knot
8. lamb
9. knit
10. wrap

Page 77
1. robin
2. hose
3. ambulance
4. violin
5. wagon
6. pot
7. puppet
8. volcano
9. desk
One Syllable: hose, pot, desk
Two Syllables: robin, wagon, puppet
Three Syllables: ambulance, violin, volcano

Page 78
1. vest
2. five
3. boat
4. zipper
5. cactus
6. kitten
7. tiger
8. octopus
9. umbrella
10. banana

Page 79
1. whale
2. frog
3. twelve
4. phone
5. clock
6. string
7. 2
8. 3
9. 1
10. 1
11. 2
12. 3

Page 80
chest, spring, ranch, light, whip, cough, wreck, stand, comb

Page 81
1. clean
2. Children
3. Dolphins
4. sprayed
5. played
6. wrote
7. Thanks
8. sang
9. laugh
10. night

Page 82
1. cheese
2. fresh
3. wheat
4. phone
5. twelve

Page 83
1. skunk
2. fruit
3. twig
4. whale
5. sheep
6. laugh
7. match
8. knee
9. knight
10. spring
11. wheel
12. branch

Page 84
1. dream
2. squash
3. peach
4. thumb
5. wheat
6. flower
7. wreath
8. twelve
9. light
10. know

Page 85
1. clock
2. shell
3. whale
4. star
5. wasp
6. tree
7. glove
8. phone
9. laugh
10. nest
11. thumb
12. chef

Page 86
1. knight
2. string
3. comb
4. wish
5. wrench
6. branch
7. cough
8. play
9. wheel
10. telephone
11. broom
12. vest

Page 87
1. jar; circle: *ar*
2. fork; circle: *or*
3. barn; circle: *ar*
4. world
5. dark
6. morning
7. far
8. north
9. worth

Page 88
1. purse
2. skirt
3. turtle
4. paper
5. circle
6. girl
7. circus
8. turn
9. burning
10. girl
11. hurt
12. certain

Page 89
1. *air*
2. *ea*
3. *are*
4. fairs
5. pears
6. share
7. wear
8. hair
9. tear

Page 90
1. Circle: near
2. Circle: peer
3. Circle: earth
4. Circle: early, hear
5. Circle: earn
6. Circle: search
7. Circle: learn
8. Circle: years, career
ear as in *beard*: near, hear, years
eer as in *cheer*: peer, career
ear as in *Earth*: earth, early, earn, search, learn

Page 91
1. circus; 2
2. evergreens; 3
3. groceries; 3
4. harbor; 2
5. bear; 1
6. feather; 2
7. important; 3
8. atmosphere; 3
9. forests; 2
10. certainly; 3

Page 92
1. forget
2. early
3. air
4. peer
5. clear
6. world
7. farm
8. dared
9. curly
10. wear

Page 93
1. cymbals
2. fry
3. cherry
4. cry
5. bicycle
6. sky
7. funny
8. penny
9. pyramid
y as long *i*: fry, cry, sky
y as long *e*: cherry, funny, penny
y as short *i*: cymbals, bicycle, pyramid

Page 94
One Syllable: cry, fry, shy
Two Syllables: rainy, sunny, system
Three Syllables: history, mystery, syllable

| 1 | 2 | 3 |
| 3 | 3 | 1 |

1. pyramid
2. Egypt
3. dry
4. why
5. royalty
6. mystery

Page 95
1. walrus; circle: *u*
2. zebra; circle: *a*
3. seven; circle: second *e*
4. wagon; circle: *o*
5. telephone; circle: second *e*
6. gerbil; circle: *i*
7. apricots; circle: *i*
8. parrot; circle: *o*
9. cactus; circle: *u*
10. president; circle: second *e*
11. canoe; circle: *a*
12. camel; circle: *e*

Answer Key
Core Skills Phonics, Grade 3

Page 96
1. eleven
2. presents
3. possible
4. science
5. problems
6. lemons
7. carrots
8. alone
9. shovel
10. album

Page 97
1. rainy
2. cherry
3. barber
4. baby
5. lion
6. fly
7. chair
8. octopus
9. panda
10. girl
11. flower
12. pearl

Page 98
1. world
2. mermaids
3. pirates
4. shy
5. search, pearls
6. windy, storm
7. year
8. tear
9. worst
10. blare

Page 99
1. under
2. surprised
3. furry
4. perch
5. squirrels
6. adult
7. canoe
8. world
9. dirt
10. worms
11. Experts
12. were

Page 100
1. more
2. year
3. garbage
4. emergency
5. worst

Page 101
1. *ei*
2. *ea*
3. *ei*
4. *ea*
5. *ei*
6. *ea*
7. *ei*
8. *ea*
9. *ei*
10. *ea*
11. *ei*
12. *ea*

Page 102
Underline: breakfast, heavy, leather, meadow, ahead, heavenly, heather, spread, weather, sweater, head, ready, pleasant
Circle: neighbor, weight, reins, neighed
1. neighbors
2. heavy
3. weight
4. meadow
5. heather

Page 103
1. wood
2. roof
3. hook
4. wool
5. raccoon
6. school
7. boot
8. pool
9. kangaroo
10. balloon
11. foot
12. spoon

Page 104
oo as in *book*: wool, took, look, stood, foot, Goodness, cooked, unhooked
oo as in *moon*: school, food, bamboo, cool, room, boots, moonlight, goose

Page 105
1. jewel
2. suit
3. newspaper
4. stew
5. chew
6. juice
7. cruise
8. few
9. blew
10. flew
11. fruit
12. juicy

Page 106
1. news
2. fruit
3. dew
4. bruised
5. juice
6. knew
7. view
8. drew
9. flew
10. blew

Page 107
1. *al*
2. *aw*
3. *al*
4. *au*
5. *aw*
6. *au*
7. *aw*
8. *al*
9. *au*
10. *aw*
11. *au*
12. *aw*

Page 108
1. always
2. autumn
3. dawn
4. call
5. crawl
6. salty
7. launch
8. shawl
9. sauce
10. saw

Page 109
Students complete the word under these pictures:
1. couch
2. house
5. spout
6. flour
7. mouth
9. cloud
12. blouse

Page 110
1. countries
2. rough
3. tough
4. trouble
5. brought
6. gourds
7. enough
8. group
9. you
10. course

Page 111
1. point
2. toys
3. soil
4. coil
5. noise
6. broil
7. oyster
8. boil
9. foil
10. flower
11. crown
12. snow

Page 112
1. enjoy
2. join
3. voyage
4. snow
5. annoy
6. oil
7. glow
8. owl
9. how
10. tower

Page 113
1. cough
2. mouse
3. hawk
4. news
5. toys
6. book
7. soup
8. fruit
9. Earth
10. jewel
11. spoon
12. owl

Page 114

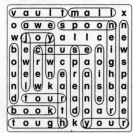

Page 115
1. thought
2. hawks
3. sauce
4. weigh
5. pour
6. brook
7. noisy
8. around
9. joyful
10. always

Page 116
1. koi
2. around
3. bought
4. baseball or ball
5. thought

Page 117
1. worm
2. coil
3. turtle
4. owl
5. stairs
6. wood
7. paw
8. deer
9. spout
10. star
11. bread
12. jewel

Page 118
1. voyage
2. four
3. forest
4. herd
5. mountains
6. walk
7. pyramids
8. cruise
9. always
10. scared

Page 119
1. cloud
2. braid
3. deer
4. coins
5. down
6. suit
7. broom
8. wall
9. clown
10. bear
11. card
12. noon

Page 120
1. purple
2. beard
3. cough
4. mouse
5. barber
6. dreary
7. weigh
8. look
9. chew
10. flower
11. saucers
12. crow